INSIDE YOU ANNUAL 2023!

D0296280

PICK YOUR WORLD CUP DREAM TEAM 40

ERLING HAALAND'S... MAN. CITY MISSION!

MATCH checks out the records Man. City striker ERLING HAALAND can break while at the club!

ERLING HAALAND 6

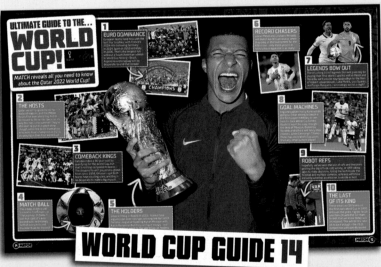

ULTIMATE GUIDE TO THE... WORLD CUP!

MATCH reveals all you need to know about the Qatar 2022 World Cup!

WORLD CUP GUIDE 14

ULTIMATE GUIDE TO... PEDRI!

MATCH tells you everything you need to know about the youngster who's already totally bossing Barcelona and Spain's midfield!

WICKED WONDERKIDS 30

EURO 2022 Scrapbook!

Last summer's Women's Euros was awesome – especially as The Lionesses made history! Check out some of the biggest moments.

EURO 2022 SCRAPBOOK 66

FOOTBALL (FINALLY) CAME HOME!

ENGLAND WOMEN won their first-ever major international tournament and lifted the nation's first trophy since 1966 at last summer's European Championship! Get in, girls!

SARINA, YOU'RE THE ONE!
England are lucky to have Sarina Wiegman in charge! The mega popular coach is one of the best in the business, proving it by lifting back-to-back Euros and becoming the first boss to win the trophy with two different nations. She also became the first manager to win her first 12 Women's Euro games!

MAGNIFICENT MEAD!
Arsenal winger Beth Mead had the month of her life! She won the Golden Boot and Player of the Tournament awards to go alongside her winners' medal! We're also shouting out to goalkeeper Mary Earps, centre-back Leah Williamson and midfielder Keira Walsh, who all made the UEFA Team of the Tournament!

SUPER SUBS!

England's squad is jam-packed with quality and that allowed Wiegman to make strong subs throughout the tournament! Alessia Russo was the star of the semi-final v Sweden with her outrageous backheel, while Ella Toone and Chloe Kelly both came on to score the all-important goals in the final against Germany!

CAPTAIN FANTASTIC!

When it was unclear whether previous captain Steph Houghton would be fit, Wiegman made the huge call to hand the armband to Arsenal star Leah Williamson! She showed awesome leadership throughout the Euros and ended her first major tournament as skipper with a trophy. It's what dreams are made of!

NOW TURN TO PAGE 66 FOR OUR EPIC EURO 2022 SCRAPBOOK!

EPIC CELEBRATIONS!

The celebrations after the final were off the charts! The players stormed Sarina Wiegman's post-match press conference singing "Football's Coming Home" and then got to party with more singing and dancing in front of 7,000 fans at Trafalgar Square in London the following day. Those memories will last forever!

WORLD CUP 2023 ULTIMATE GUIDE!

FIFA WOMEN'S WORLD CUP

AU 20 NZ 23

MATCH gives you the lowdown on the 2023 Women's World Cup in New Zealand and Australia...

THE HOSTS!

Not only will the 2023 Women's World Cup be the first to be held in Oceania and the first to be co-hosted by two nations, it'll also be the first to be expanded from 24 to 32 teams. We're so pumped!

THE HOLDERS!

The United States are the defending champions having won the previous two tournaments back in 2015 and 2019! As the top-ranked nation in the world going in to 2023, they're sure to be favourites again!

THE STARS!

The Netherlands' Vivianne Miedema, Spain's Alexia Putellas, USA's Rose Lavelle and Brazil's Debinha are our players to watch - plus Chelsea striker Sam Kerr, who'll be playing in her home nation Australia!

THE STADIUMS!

The tournament will be played across five cities and six stadiums in Australia, and four cities and four venues in New Zealand! The largest is Stadium Australia in Sydney, which will pack in over 80,000 fans!

THE LIONESSES!

England will go into the tournament as European champions - how good does that sound? They'll have more or less the same squad and will need to draw from all of their winning experience to make history again!

ERLING HAALAND'S...

MAN. CITY MISSION!

MATCH checks out the records MAN. CITY striker ERLING HAALAND will have his eyes on while at the club!

ALL-TIME TOP SCORER!

RECORD: SERGIO AGUERO ★ 260 GOALS

Sergio Aguero scored 260 goals in his ten-year spell at the club in all competitions, leaving as Man. City's all-time top scorer at the end of the 2020-21 campaign! If Haaland can better Kun's record, he'll deserve a statue outside the Etihad as well!

MOST PREMIER LEAGUE GOALS!

RECORD: SERGIO AGUERO ★ 184 GOALS

Let's say Haaland emulates Aguero by spending a decade in the Premier League... he's gonna have to average 19 goals every season to better the Argentina legend's Prem goal record! That might sound doable, but it all depends on injuries – and whether the Norwegian stays that long!

DID YOU KNOW?

Lionesses right-back Lucy Bronze is just the second English woman to play for Barcelona in the history of the club after Toni Duggan, who also turned out for Atletico Madrid!

FOOTY FLASHBACK

...to when Spain left-back Marcos Alonso used to play for Bolton Wanderers in the Championship! He spent three years there after signing from Real Madrid, before playing for Fiorentina, Sunderland and then Chelsea!

SAY WHAT?

Liverpool forward Luis Diaz's dog is named after Real Madrid legend Toni Kroos! Although we're not sure if that changed after Los Blancos edged out The Reds 1-0 in the 2022 Champions League final...

GOALS IN A SINGLE SEASON!
RECORD: SERGIO AGUERO ★ 26 GOALS
As lethal as Aguero was, he never managed to break the 30-goal barrier in the Prem. In his three seasons in the Bundesliga, Haaland's best tally was 27 strikes from 28 games in 2020-21! He definitely would have reached 30 if it weren't for injuries...

NORWEGIAN WITH MOST GAMES!
RECORD: ALF-INGE HAALAND ★ 47 GAMES
Haaland is the sixth Norwegian to play for Man. City in the history of the club! His dad Alf-Inge currently holds the record for the Norwegian with the most appearances, but he's bound to overtake his dad very soon!

GOALS IN EUROPEAN COMPS!
RECORD: SERGIO AGUERO ★ 43 GOALS
We already know that Haaland absolutely loves playing in the Champions League! He became the first teenager to score in five consecutive Champo League matches at RB Salzburg and then won the CL Golden Boot at Borussia Dortmund in 2020-21!

FREAK INJURIES!

After Hartlepool's MARK SHELTON was ruled out in 2022 for shoving a cotton bud too far down his ear, MATCH looks back on some of footy's weirdest injuries...

ALEX STEPNEY

Way back in 1975, Man. United goalkeeper Alex Stepney dislocated his jaw while shouting instructions to his defenders. Ouch!

DARREN BARNARD

Former Wales international Darren Barnard slipped on his puppy's poo and was out for five months with a ruptured ankle ligament!

DAVE BEASANT

The ex-England goalie dropped a bottle of salad cream in his kitchen and attempted to control it with his foot. He was out for eight weeks!

DARIUS VASSELL

The striker bizarrely decided to self-operate on a blood blister on his foot with a power drill! Unsurprisingly, it didn't end very well...

DAVID JAMES

The ex-England, Liverpool, West Ham, Man. City and Portsmouth goalkeeper once pulled a muscle in his back when reaching for the TV remote control!

CHARLIE GEORGE

Arsenal's 1971 FA Cup hero accidentally cut off his index finger with a lawnmower while he was cutting the grass. Now that's gotta hurt!

LION CUB!

Top-quality Three Lions winger Jarrod Bowen posted this LOL childhood snap on his Instagram page after he was handed his first senior England call-up in 2022. Total legend!

MAGIC MEAD!
Nobody has scored more goals at a single Women's Euros than lethal England winger Beth Mead's six strikes at Euro 2022! For more on how the Lionesses made footy history, turn to page 66!

BANNER BURN!
After Switzerland finished above Italy in qualifying for the 2022 World Cup, this Swiss fan created one of the most savage banners we've seen in a long time! Top marks for originality!

IS GARETH BALE...
BRITAIN'S BEST-EVER PLAYER?

BRILLIANT BALE!

The former Southampton academy product's awesome career has seen him transform from a left-back who failed to win any of his first 24 games in a Tottenham shirt to one of the finest British forwards of all time! MATCH reckons it's time to settle the debate as to whether Bale deserves to be crowned Britain's GOAT or not...

OF COURSE HE'S BRITAIN'S BEST!

✓ Bale lifted three La Ligas and four Champions League trophies during his time at Real Madrid, performing a jaw-dropping overhead-kick versus Liverpool in the 2018 final and scoring a solo stunner against Barca in the 2014 Copa del Rey final!

✓ He's been an inspirational talisman for Wales throughout his jaw-dropping international career, providing some really special performances in the biggest games, and will retire as his nation's all-time top goalscorer and appearance maker!

✓ Before joining Real Madrid for a world-record transfer fee he was Tottenham's best player, winning the Premier League's Player of the Season prize in 2013 after bagging 21 goals in 33 games!

NAH, HE'S OVERRATED!

✗ He's wasted way too much of the latter part of his career benchwarming at Real Madrid, and sometimes seems more motivated by his golf handicap score than tearing up the football pitch for his club!

✗ He's spent way too much time injured on the treatment table and has only played 30+ league games in four of the last 14 league campaigns for Real Madrid and Tottenham! He's too fragile!

✗ There's no doubting that he's a special player, but there are other British footballers who have had better all-round careers or who were more technically gifted!

MATCH! MAD!

When we caught up with Tottenham and Wales star Ben Davies, he revealed that he was a huge MATCH fan growing up! He used to buy the magazine with his pocket money every week. Ledge!

MERSEYSIDE MASCOT!

Everton's hero of 2022 was arguably Myra the dog, who became The Toffees' lucky mascot after she was paraded through a crowd of fans before their win over Chelsea at Goodison Park!

FASHION FAIL!

Somebody call the fashion police, we've got an emergency! England ace Kalvin Phillips was spotted wearing what we can only presume are two enormous Cornish pasties. LOL!

I'M DEFINITELY NUMBER ONE!

Scan the QR code now to vote for whether you think Gareth Bale is Britain's greatest-ever player!

THE OTHER CONTENDERS!

These players also could be considered Britain's greatest!

GEORGE BEST
Country: N. Ireland ✦ Caps/Goals: 37/9

He didn't win as many honours but his technique and dribbling skills were so good Pele said he could've been Brazilian!

BOBBY CHARLTON
Country: England ✦ Caps/Goals: 106/49

The goalscoring midfielder and Man. United legend was one of the main reasons why England won the 1966 World Cup!

KENNY DALGLISH
Country: Scotland ✦ Caps/Goals: 102/30

"King Kenny" is regarded as the greatest player Celtic have ever produced and one of Liverpool's best players of all time!

RYAN GIGGS
Country: Wales ✦ Caps/Goals: 64/12

Some fans think Bale isn't even the best-ever Welsh player, as that title belongs to the former Manchester United winger!

WAYNE ROONEY
Country: England ✦ Caps/Goals: 120/53

Wazza retired as England and Man. United's all-time top scorer, while no outfielder has won more Three Lions caps than him either!

FOOTY DEBATES!

Have your say on these other top footy debates by ticking your winner in these head-to-head battles!

KLOPP		GUARDIOLA
	V	

RONALDO		MESSI
	V	

PREMIER LEAGUE		CHAMPO LEAGUE
	V	

ADIDAS		NIKE
	V	

SERIE A		LA LIGA
	V	

FOOTBALL MANAGER 2022 — FM FREAK!

Polish "gaffer" Pawel Sicinski set a new Guinness World Record in 2022 for the longest single game of Football Manager! He played 416 seasons and won 1,258 trophies, simming only 260 days. We're not sure if we're impressed or worried!

HE SAID WHAT?

"IMPOSSIBLE! DURING THE GAME I WOULD PUNCH AT LEAST TWO PLAYERS AND AFTER THE GAME EIGHT!"

Zlatan Ibrahimovic gave this response to being asked if he was planning to become a manager when he retired...

YOUNG LIONS ROAR!

ENGLAND's Under-19 side won the EUROPEAN CHAMPIONSHIP in 2022 and are hoping for further glory at the 2023 Under-20 WORLD CUP! We pick out some stars to watch...

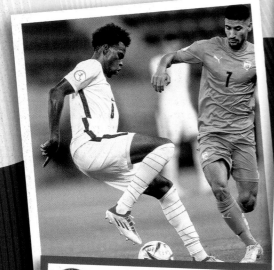

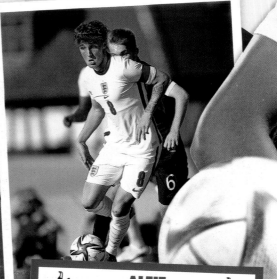

CARNEY CHUKWUEMEKA

Position: Midfielder Age: 18

Carney was born in Austria, but grew up in Northampton and joined Aston Villa's awesome academy at the age of 12! He was England's star player and top scorer at the European Championship with three goals, including one in the final in extra-time! He's probably the most experienced baller after playing 11 PL games for Villa in 2021-22, and joined Chelsea for £20 million last summer!

BROOKE NORTON-CUFFY

Position: Right-back Age: 18

The pacy and powerful right-back joined Arsenal when he was 12 years old and has risen through the youth ranks! He was named The Gunners' Scholar of the Year in 2022 after impressing on loan at League One Lincoln and played in every game of England Under-19s' run to the Euros trophy last summer! Some Arsenal supporters have even compared him to Man. City magician Joao Cancelo!

ALFIE DEVINE

Position: Midfielder Age: 18

Devine grew up in the rugby league stronghold of St. Helens and his dad played professionally, but Alfie always wanted to play footy! He was released by Liverpool when he was 11 years old before joining Wigan. From there, he was signed by Spurs in 2020 and became the club's youngest first teamer when he featured - and scored - in an FA Cup tie against Marine in January 2021!

RECORD ATTENDANCES!

Loads of new record attendances were set in the women's game in 2022! Check out these awesome stats...

91,648

Barcelona and Wolfsburg's Champions League clash at the Nou Camp broke the world record attendance for a women's match. Wow!

87,192

The Women's Euro 2022 final broke the 58-year record attendance at a Euros tournament - including men's matches!

SCARLETT LOVES TO RIP NET!

THE BEST OF THE REST!

JARELL QUANSAH
Position: Centre-back   Age: 19

The ball-playing defender scored England's Euros semi-final winner against Italy and has been in The Reds' academy since he was five!

HARVEY VALE
Position: Midfielder   Age: 19

The Chelsea youngster captained England to glory at last summer's Euros as a left wing-back, but prefers to play as an attacking midfielder!

AARON RAMSEY
Position: Midfielder   Age: 19

Another class Aston Villa academy graduate, Ramsey will be hoping a loan spell at Norwich will help him develop like older brother Jacob!

LIAM DELAP
Position: Forward   Age: 19

The son of ex-Republic of Ireland international Rory Delap has played for Man. City's first team and scored on his debut in the League Cup!

JAMIE BYNOE-GITTENS
Position: Winger   Age: 18

A London-born tricky winger who was initially on the books of Man. City before moving to Germany to play for Borussia Dortmund!

DANE SCARLETT
Position: Striker   Age: 18

The lethal young finisher led the line for England at the Euros and scored some vital goals! He's been tipped for the top by both Jose Mourinho and Antonio Conte, with the Portuguese gaffer handing him his Premier League debut in 2021 and the Italian including him in first-team training throughout the 2021-22 season. He'd love to follow in Harry Kane's footsteps at Spurs!

JAMES WARD-PROWSE'S FREE-KICK TIPS!

JAMES WARD-PROWSE is one of the Prem's best-ever free-kick takers, and he gave MATCH some tips in mastering set-pieces...

PREPARATION!
JAMES SAYS: "For my technique I try to keep everything the same. I place the ball in the same position, with the logo facing the same way, take four steps back, and then try to picture where I want the ball to go!"

MY TECHNIQUE!
JAMES SAYS: "I've done a lot of repetition to find my own technique which works for me. I hit the ball with both feet off the ground, because it helps to get the ball up and over the wall, and gives it momentum on the other side!"

ROLE MODELS!
JAMES SAYS: "I've tried to take bits from different players – Steven Gerrard was good at free-kicks and so was Frank Lampard, but he was more about power. My style's more like David Beckham's, but you have to find your own technique!"

KEEP ON PRACTISING!
JAMES SAYS: "It's obvious, but you just have to get a bag of balls and keep practising. The more you can repeat it, the more likely you'll be able to do it in a game! It's all about repetition and getting the pictures in your head of how it'll go!"

FIND YOUR STYLE!
JAMES SAYS: "You've got to find what works for you. Experiment with different things and once you've found a style you're comfortable with, keep working at it!"

49,094

WSL giants Chelsea and Man. City broke the record attendance for the final of the FA Women's Cup at Wembley!

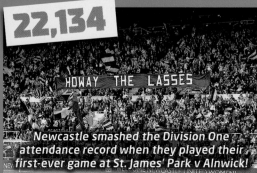

22,134

HOWAY THE LASSES

Newcastle smashed the Division One attendance record when they played their first-ever game at St. James' Park v Alnwick!

8,004

The Women's League Cup final also had a new record attendance at Plough Lane between Chelsea and Man. City!

WIN PRIZES!

NACON CONTROLLER!

Thanks to our top mates at Nacon, you can take your gaming to the next level! We've got seven of their top-quality Pro Compact Controllers for Xbox to give away. Get in there!

7 PRIZES!

Available in black or white, the cool wired Pro Compact Controller is designed for Xbox Series X|S, Xbox One and Windows 10 PC!

The Pro Compact Controller is 15% smaller than a classic game controller to fit a wide range of hand sizes, while its textured grip ensures comfort and stability during long gaming sessions!

In addition to offering the classic features of the Xbox Wireless Controller, a dedicated app available on the Microsoft Store gives access to the advanced mode settings to create your own game profile!

Xbox console not included as part of the prize and for illustration purposes only.

 **nacon**

For more info on this incredible controller and more cool gaming accessories, head over to nacongaming.com and follow @Nacon

CLOSING DATE: JAN. 31 2023

HOW TO ENTER! ➤ WWW.MATCHFOOTBALL.CO.UK

Then click 'Win' in the navigation bar on the MATCH website. Full T&Cs are available online.

XAVI

1 In what year did the legendary midfielder make his senior debut for Spain - 1990, 1996, 2000 or 2004?

2 True or False? He was named Euro 2008's Player of the Tournament in Austria and Switzerland!

3 The Barcelona legend helped Spain lift the 2010 World Cup, but did he score a goal in South Africa?

4 How many assists did he register in the 2012 European Championship final versus Italy - none, two or three?

5 He often played alongside Andres Iniesta, but who finished with more Spain caps - Xavi or Iniesta?

ANSWERS ON PAGE 94

ULTIMATE GUIDE TO THE...
WORLD CUP!

FIFA WORLD CUP Qatar 2022
Match Schedule

MATCH reveals all you need to know about the Qatar 2022 World Cup!

1 EURO DOMINANCE

European teams have now won the last four trophies, with France's 2018 title following Germany in 2014, Spain in 2010 and Italy in 2006. That's the longest run without a South American winner in World Cup history – Brazil, Argentina and Uruguay will be desperate to end that streak!

2 THE HOSTS

Qatar weren't popular hosts for loads of reasons, and the Middle East's first-ever World Cup had to be moved to the winter because it's way too hot in the summer! They're still keen to put on a good show though, while the team themselves, who were Asian champions in 2019, are playing in their first World Cup!

3 COMEBACK KINGS

Canada ended a 36-year wait by qualifying for this World Cup, but that's nothing compared to Wales – The Dragons haven't played at a global finals since 1958, 64 years ago! Both teams have exciting stars, and they'll be desperate to make a big impact!

4 MATCH BALL

The adidas Al Rihla ball translates from Arabic as 'The Journey'. It doesn't just look cool, it's also packed with technology so that every kick and movement can be tracked!

5 THE HOLDERS

Since winning in Russia in 2018, France have arguably got even stronger, winning the last UEFA Nations League and pairing Kylian Mbappe with Karim Benzema! But they can't get sloppy – last time Les Bleus went to the World Cup as holders in 2002, they were dumped out in the groups!

6 RECORD CHASERS

Lionel Messi and Cristiano Ronaldo will match World Cup records when they play at the tournament for the fifth time - only three players in history have appeared in as many!

7 LEGENDS BOW OUT

There's a long list of legends that will probably be playing their final World Cups! As well as Messi and Ronaldo, we'll also be saying goodbye to the likes of Robert Lewandowski, Luka Modric, Luis Suarez and Sergio Busquets - who will go out on a high?

8 GOAL MACHINES

England captain Harry Kane will be going to Qatar aiming to become the first player in history to win back-to-back World Cup Golden Boots! It won't be easy, though - the likes of Mbappe, Benzema, Ronaldo and others will fancy their chances, while Germany's Thomas Muller has more World Cup goals than any other current player!

9 ROBOT REFS

Hopefully we've seen the last of refs and linesmen getting the big offside calls wrong, or VAR taking ages to make decisions. Using the tech inside the football and multiple cameras, referees will know instantly whether an attacker is onside or not!

10 THE LAST OF ITS KIND

There were just 13 teams at the first-ever World Cup in 1930, and over the years it grew to 16 and then 24 until the 32-team format that we know today was introduced. This will be the last of its kind though - the 2026 competition will have 48 teams!

WORLD CUP 2022... STADIUM GUIDE!

MATCH reveals the jaw-dropping stadiums that'll be used in Qatar...

AHMAD BIN ALI STADIUM

City: Al Rayyan
Capacity: 44,740

Usually the Ahmad Bin Ali Stadium is home to Al Rayyan, the Qatari club that Colombia star James Rodriguez plays for, but on November 29 it'll host the mega clash between England and Wales!

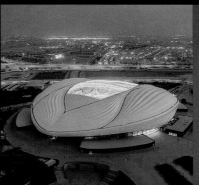

AL JANOUB STADIUM

City: Al Wakrah
Capacity: 40,000

If the Arab Cup is anything to go by, this ground could see epic drama - of the six games that it hosted, five had goals in the 87th minute or later! France's World Cup defence begins here against Australia!

LUSAIL ICONIC STADIUM

City: Lusail ★ **Capacity:** 80,000

This is where the final takes place and although the 80,000 seats will be packed with fans for the big day on December 18, loads of them will be taken out again and given to developing countries once the tournament is all over!

STADIUM 974

City: Doha
Capacity: 40,000

This cool-looking ground is called Stadium 974 because that's how many shipping containers were used to build it! Once the World Cup is finished, the temporary venue will be taken down!

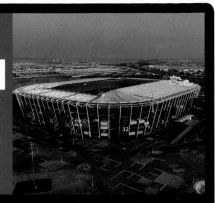

KHALIFA INTERNATIONAL STADIUM

City: Al Rayyan ★ **Capacity:** 45,416

England's World Cup campaign begins against Iran on November 21 in the oldest ground being used in Qatar. The Khalifa was first built in 1976, and used to host all the country's major sporting events!

EDUCATION CITY STADIUM

City: Al Rayyan ★ **Capacity:** 45,350

The "Diamond in the Desert", as it's known, was one of the grounds that was tested out during the FIFA Arab Cup in 2021. Asian giants South Korea will play all of their Group H games here!

AL BAYT STADIUM

City: Al Khor
Capacity: 60,000

This ground will host some big games, including the hosts' first-ever World Cup match, Germany v Spain and one of the semi-finals! With a retractable roof, it should stay cool under the roasting Qatar sun!

AL THUMAMA STADIUM

City: Doha
Capacity: 40,000

This is where the tournament begins, as African champions Senegal meet the Netherlands on November 21! The ultra-cool designed is based on the traditional Arabic headwear, the Gahfiya!

THE GREATEST WORLD CUP GOALS EVER!

Take a look at some of the greatest and most famous net-busters in World Cup history!

 GEOFF HURST

1966 England v West Germany

As the goal that sealed England's first and only World Cup trophy, this is undoubtedly the most important goal in the history of English footy! And it sealed an incredible hat-trick for Geoff Hurst - the only player to ever do so in a World Cup final! The commentary is legendary, too - "Some people are on the pitch, they think it's all over... it is now!"

QR CODES EXPLAINED

This is a QR code – just scan it with your phone or tablet to watch each video clip on YouTube. Here's how to do it:

Download and install a free QR Code reader from the app or android store.

Hold your phone or tablet over the QR code and you'll be sent to the clip. Easy!

CARLOS ALBERTO

1970 Brazil v Italy

This is possibly the best team goal ever! Brazil were already bossing the 1970 World Cup final when they put together this slick passing move, finished off with a bullet shot from their captain to make it 4-1!

SAEED AL OWAIRAN

1994 Saudi Arabia v Belgium

Some players get remembered for just one thing only, like Saeed Al Owairan! The Saudi Arabia midfielder picked up the ball in his own half and went on a crazy, mazy run before scoring. Sick solo effort!

MANUEL NEGRETE

1986 Mexico v Bulgaria

This is one of the coolest one-twos ever! Negrete chips it up to his team-mate who volleys it delicately back to him, before the Mexico star bicycle kicks it past Bulgarian keeper Borislav Mihaylov. Class!

▶ ARCHIE GEMMILL

1978 Scotland v Netherlands

Scotland fans should enjoy watching this! Gemmill's brilliant dribble through the Dutch defence and wicked finish is probably the most famous World Cup goal in Scottish footy history. Worldie alert!

▶ NACER CHADLI

2018 Belgium v Japan

You won't see a better counter-attacking goal than this one! Thibaut Courtois catches a Japan corner and within ten seconds the ball is in the back of the net at the other end!

▶ TIM CAHILL

2014 Australia v Netherlands

The Socceroos' all-time record scorer caught this volley absolutely perfectly – and it's an even better strike when you realise that he's not even left-footed. Wow!

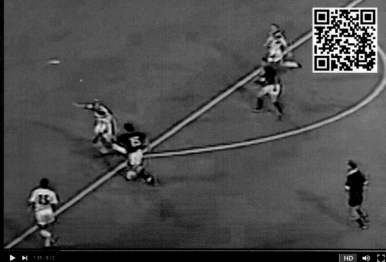

▶ DIEGO MARADONA

1986 Argentina v England

Maradona's display against England is probably the most famous individual performance ever! He'd already scored once with his hand when he took on the entire Three Lions team and slotted home!

▶ ROBERTO BAGGIO

1990 Italy v Czechoslovakia

Scoring a goal like this at a home World Cup is the stuff dreams are made of! Baggio played a one-two on the halfway line before waltzing though the Czech defence to notch an absolute solo stunner!

▶ ESTEBAN CAMBIASSO

2006 Argentina v Serbia & Montenegro

Cambiasso might have got the final touch, but this goal was all about the team! All but two Argentina players were involved in this jaw-dropping 25-pass move, before the midfielder poked home!

▶ MICHAEL OWEN

1998 England v Argentina

The England striker was only 18 when he absolutely tore the Argentina defence apart! After burning past them with his unreal pace, he calmly placed the ball into the top corner with a slick finish!

▶ MAXI RODRIGUEZ

2006 Argentina v Mexico

Argentina struck some absolute bangers at this World Cup! This one wasn't a flowing passing move though, it was a mind-blowing chest-trap and unstoppable 25-yard volley!

▶ DENNIS BERGKAMP

1998 Netherlands v Argentina

This goal wasn't just a moment of absolute genius from ex-Arsenal legend Bergkamp, who produced a world-class first touch and finish, it was also a 90th-minute winner in a tense World Cup quarter-final!

▶ BENJAMIN PAVARD

2018 France v Argentina

If the best striker in the world buried this half-volley with the outside of his boot we'd still be talking about it today, but Pavard is a defender – there's no way he should be burying goals with technique this good!

▶ FABIO QUAGLIARELLA

2010 Italy v Slovakia

You don't often see keepers getting chipped from this far out, but Quagliarella had a habit of doing spectacular things! It wasn't enough for Italy to avoid defeat and crashing out in the group stage, though!

▶ GIOVANNI V. BRONCKHORST

2010 Netherlands v Uruguay

Back when the Rangers manager was still a player, he helped fire his country into the World Cup final with one of the hardest shots you'll ever see! It came out of absolutely nowhere and hit the top corner!

▶ ROBIN VAN PERSIE

2014 Netherlands v Spain

We only had room for one header in this list, and it had to be this one! The Spanish defence had no way of stopping RVP's genius improvised diving-header finish!

▶ LIONEL MESSI

2014 Argentina v Bosnia & Herzegovina

No list would be complete without this guy! This goal is classic Messi – he dribbles past one defender, plays a one-two, dribbles past some more defenders, then nails his finish into the corner off the post!

▶ JAMES RODRIGUEZ

2014 Colombia v Uruguay

James won the FIFA Puskas Goal of the Year award and bagged a move to Real Madrid after this incredible strike! He popped the ball up with his chest and unleashed a left-footed volley from miles out!

THE ROAD TO THE...
WORLD CUP!

Grab a dice and some coins to use as counters, and take on your pals in our wicked board game! Can you make it all the way to the World Cup trophy?

START ▶	2 ▶	3 ▶	4 ▶	5 ▶	6 ▶
KICK-OFF! The player who rolls the highest number goes first!			**LEGEND!** You impress on trial and sign for a League Two club! Move forward two spaces! LEAGUE TWO | EFL		

◀ 12	◀ 11	◀ 10	◀ 9	◀ 8	◀ 7
FAIL! You miss a sitter in a top-of-the-table clash! Move back one space!			**LEGEND!** A League One club snaps you up! Move forward two spaces! LEAGUE ONE | EFL		**FAIL!** Your first season ends in disappointment and you get released! Move back five spaces!

13 ▶	14 ▶	15 ▶	16 ▶	17 ▶	18 ▶
	LEGEND! Your team bags promotion to the Championship! Move forward two spaces! CHAMPIONSHIP | EFL			**FAIL!** You pick up an injury in training and get ruled out for six weeks! Move back two spaces!	

◀ 24	◀ 23	◀ 22	◀ 21	◀ 20	◀ 19
		LEGEND! You bag the winner in the play-off final! Move forward four spaces!			**LEGEND!** You score a worldy against Liverpool in an FA Cup clash! Move forward one space!

25 ▶	26 ▶	27 ▶	28 ▶	29 ▶	30 ▶
FAIL! The manager sends you back to the Championship on loan! Move back five places!		**LEGEND!** You're named the Premier League Player of the Month! Move forward two spaces!	**LEGEND!** Your epic form earns you an international call-up! Move forward four spaces!		**FAIL!** The fans turn on you after saying you want to leave! Move back one space!

◀ 36	◀ 35	◀ 34	◀ 33	◀ 32	◀ 31
	LEGEND! The fans come up with an awesome chant for you! Move forward one space!		**LEGEND!** You're named in the World Cup squad! Move forward one space!		**LEGEND!** You bag a move to a team in the Champions League! Move forward three spaces!

37 ▶	38 ▶	39 ▶	40 ▶	41 ▶	WINNER!
LEGEND! You score a hat-trick in the World Cup! Move forward two spaces!			**FAIL!** You are sent off in the World Cup group stage! Move back one space!	**FAIL!** You miss a penalty in the World Cup final! Move back five spaces!	**YOU'RE A FOOTY LEGEND!** YOU'VE WON THE WORLD CUP!

BECKHAM

1 True or False? The legendary England midfielder's first-ever Three Lions goal was a 30-yard free-kick!

2 Name the iconic 2002 film starring actress Keira Knightley that had Beckham's name in its title!

3 How many times did he captain The Three Lions during his 115 international appearances – 30, 59, 80 or 100?

4 He helped England qualify for the 2002 World Cup thanks to a last-gasp free-kick against which Euro nation?

5 Who's the only outfielder to have won more England caps than Becks – Wayne Rooney or Steven Gerrard?

ANSWERS ON PAGE 94 →

GOAL KING #1
KANE

FACTPACK!

Club: *Tottenham*
Country: *England*
Age: *29*
Height: *6ft 2in*
Top Skill: *Unstoppable shooting!*

HARRY KANE has been banging in goals for years now and is well on his way to breaking **ENGLAND**, **TOTTENHAM** and Premier League records. Legend!

GOALSCORING GAME

✓ Kane's one of the best finishers on the planet because he always smashes the ball with so much power - whether he's using his left or right foot!

✓ Kane's link-up play allows him to form deadly partnerships, too! Hazza and Son Heung-min are always setting each other up to score!

✓ He's also one of the best penalty-takers around! He hardly ever misses, and if he does - like he did v Denmark at Euro 2020 - he often nets the rebound!

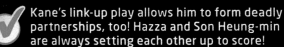
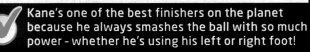
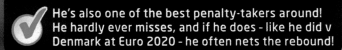

BEST SEASON

The 2017-18 campaign was the highest-scoring season of Kane's career, with 30 goals in the Premier League and 41 in all comps! He also bagged seven Champions League goals, but Spurs crashed out in the last 16 to Juventus after winning a group involving Real Madrid!

LAST SEASON

It took a while for Kane to find his feet during the 2021-22 campaign – he was still tired after firing England to the final of Euro 2020! His first Premier League goal didn't arrive until October, yet he still ended up with 17 PL goals and 27 in all comps!

GREATEST GOAL

Tottenham	4	1	Crystal Palace

March 7, 2021 Kane's scored some sick goals during his career – including some stunners v deadly rivals Arsenal – but this is one of the best! He whipped the ball into the top bins first time from 25 yards out!

STAT PACK

39 In 2017, Kane smashed in 39 Premier League goals – a record for a single calendar year!

6 At the 2018 World Cup, Kane won the Golden Boot after bagging six goals. Hero!

50 In June 2022, he scored his 50th England goal – three short of Wayne Rooney's all-time record!

3 Before 2022-23, he needed just five Prem goals to move into third in the all-time top scorers list!

WHAT'S NEXT?

Despite his epic goalscoring ability, Kane has never won a major trophy, losing in four different finals with both England and Tottenham! He's absolutely desperate to end that losing streak, while he could also become the first-ever player to win two World Cup Golden Boots!

Stats correct up to start of the 2022-23 season.

BIG MATCH QUIZ!

How many of these ace Premier League teasers can you get right?

SPOT THE BALL!

Mark where you think the ball is in this Aston Villa v Crystal Palace pic!

FIVE-A-SIDE!

Can you work out which players are in this epic Prem five-a-side team?

1. GK: Poland keeper who's played for West Ham and Arsenal!

2. DF: No-nonsense Argentina ace whose nickname is 'Cuti'!

3. RMF: Captain of Norway and a tricky five-star skiller!

4. LMF: Zambian midfielder who joined Brighton in 2021!

5. ST: Tall Kiwi whose surname is a type of material!

the price is right!

Match the stars with the money their current club splashed out on them!

1 — Edouard Mendy, Chelsea

2 — Ben Godfrey, Everton

3 — Adam Armstrong, Southampton

A — £25 million

B — £22 million

C — £15 million

KIT CLASH!

Which Wolves attacker has been photoshopped onto a Man. United kit?

ACE ACTIVITY

FACE IN THE CROWD

Spot the ten Premier League stars hiding somewhere in the crowd!

Trent Alexander-Arnold

Joao Cancelo

Jarrod Bowen

Marc Guehi

Ivan Toney

Stuart Dallas

Eric Dier

Bruno Guimaraes

Harvey Barnes

Leandro Trossard

MATCH'S... Crystal Ball! 2023!

We've taken a look into our crystal ball to predict what could happen in 2023!

Mbappe player-manager!

Fed up of having to listen to his manager barking orders, Kylian Mbappe takes the executive decision to make himself player manager of PSG! In his first press conference as gaffer of the French giants, he immediately names himself captain and demands the club signs his best mate Ousmane Dembele from Barcelona!

Magpies sign Messi!

After turning 36 years old in June 2023, Lionel Messi decides it's finally time to give the Premier League a chance! The likes of Man. City, Man. United, Chelsea and Liverpool offer him a season-long contract, but the Argentina legend says his "childhood dream" was always to wear the black and white stripes of Newcastle, where he's given a £300-million-a-year contract!

Norwich's new mascot!

After gaining promotion once again to the Premier League in 2022-23, the big Norwich bosses decide to celebrate by creating a new club mascot to replace Captain Canary! They hold a competition to give fans the chance to create and vote for their favourite, with "Mr Yo-Yo" chosen as the winner to represent their constant back-and-forth to the

Ronaldo's statue shocker!

Man. United decide to honour Cristiano Ronaldo's legacy at the club with a statue outside Old Trafford! In a controversial move, they decide to put his head on a body of a goat to represent his greatest-of-all-time status, but it quickly gets removed after Cristiano complains that the animal was "lacking a defined six-pack"!

Birth certificate crazies!

In pre-season training for the 2023-24 season, James Milner once again wins the annual bleep test! Club doctors and scientists can't work out how the 37-year-old keeps beating the club's fittest youngsters and discover a typo on his birth certificate that says he was born in 1996 instead of 1986 – making him ten years younger than they thought!

ZIDANE

1 He scored twice in the 1998 World Cup final against which huge nation – Argentina, Italy, Germany or Brazil?

2 What was the legendary France playmaker's famous nickname – Zidou, Zizoo, Zizou or Zishoe?

3 True or False? The former Real Madrid, Juventus, Bordeaux and Cannes star was also eligible to play for Morocco!

4 Which famous adidas boots did he used to wear during his playing days – Nemeziz, X or Predator?

5 How many international goals did he score in his 108 appearances for Les Bleus – 21, 31, 41 or 51?

ANSWERS ON PAGE 94 ➤

ULTIMATE GUIDE TO...
PEDRI!

FAST FACTS

TEENAGE TEARAWAY
Pedri was only 16 when he made his debut for his first pro club, Las Palmas, in August 2019. A month later he became the club's youngest-ever goalscorer!

BARCA BREAKTHROUGH
Barca signed Pedri in July 2020 and, although he was still a teenager, he quickly became a key man and only missed one league game in his first season!

EURO 2020 STAR
Pedri settled into the Spain team just as quickly as he did at Barca, and rocked at Euro 2020. He was Young Player of the Tournament as La Roja reached the semi-finals!

INJURY SETBACK
After the Euros, Pedri went to the Olympics where he played his 73rd game of the season! It wasn't a surprise that his 2021-22 campaign was ruined by injury - but he's ready to rule again!

MATCH tells you everything you need to know about the youngster who's already totally bossing Barcelona and Spain's midfield!

FOOTY BRAIN
Pedri doesn't turn 21 until the end of 2023, but he plays like a guy who's been bossing midfields for years! When he's got the ball he almost always makes the right decision, plus he's got the versatility and intelligence to play in a number of roles!

2021-22 LA LIGA STATS
Games: 12
Goals: 3
Assists: 1

CLASS PASSING

Both Barcelona and Spain love to keep possession, so to play in midfield for them you have to be a world-class passer – and that's exactly what Pedri is! Whether he's keeping it short, playing it long or threading a defence-splitting through-ball, he has laser-like accuracy!

FAST FEET

Opposition midfielders hate coming up against Pedri because he's almost impossible to get the ball off. As well as his top-class passing range, he can always wriggle out of any tight spot with his dribbling ability, jaw-dropping technique and quick bursts of acceleration. Hero!

IS HE THE NEXT... ANDRES INIESTA?

Iniesta was one of the greatest midfielders of all time, winning Champions League titles with Barcelona and the World Cup and Euros with Spain, so if Pedri's career is only half as good he'll be unreal! He plays in the same style as the Barca legend, and recently took his famous No.8 shirt!

FACTFILE!
Club: *Barcelona*
Age: *19*
Position: *Midfielder*
Boots: *adidas Copa Sense+*

PEDRI'S PALS!

Pedri isn't the only young superstar at the Nou Camp!

GAVI
Midfielder

If Pedri is like Iniesta, then Gavi is like another Barca midfield legend, Xavi! With the ex-skipper now managing the club, the 18-year-old has the perfect coach!

NICO GONZALEZ
Midfielder

The Spanish giants' trio of homegrown midfielders with bright futures is completed by Nico. He's a classy DM who will, in the future, replace Sergio Busquets!

ANSU FATI
Winger

Barca's youngest-ever player has had a tough few years with injuries, but he's got huge potential. He's so highly rated, the club gave him the No.10 shirt after Lionel Messi left!

RONALD ARAUJO
Defender

The Uruguayan is already a Barca regular, and looks to have a big future at the Nou Camp. The club will need a top class centre-back when Gerard Pique retires!

NOW TURN OVER FOR LOADS MORE WICKED WONDERKIDS!

THE NEXT GEN

FLORIAN WIRTZ

Position: Att. midfielder
Age: 19 ★ Club: B. Leverkusen

Wirtz stunned German footy when he became the youngest player in top-flight history back in 2020, and a month later he became the youngest goalscorer too! The teenager is already Leverkusen's main midfield playmaker – last season he got ten Bundesliga assists, more than any other teenager in Europe's top five leagues!

IS HE THE NEXT... KAI HAVERTZ?

Wirtz replaced Havertz as Leverkusen's youngest-ever player, and has replaced him in their XI too! His next challenge is to fully recover from his ACL injury and become a regular alongside Kai in the national team!

YOUSSOUFA MOUKOKO

Position: Striker
Age: 17 ★ Club: B. Dortmund

Moukoko made his Bundesliga bow the day after turning 16 to become the league's new youngest player, and within a few weeks he'd become the youngest scorer and youngest Champions League player too! He hit six goals on his Dortmund U19s debut when he was still only 14, and went on to bag 141 goals in just 88 matches!

IS HE THE NEXT... ERLING HAALAND?

With an insane goalscoring record at a young age, a lethal left foot and a spot in Dortmund's line-up, the comparisons are obvious! Don't be shocked to see Moukoko follow Haaland to the Prem one day too!

RYAN GRAVENBERCH

Position: Midfielder
Age: 20 ★ Club: Bayern Munich

Gravenberch is one of those players that every club in Europe has been watching for the last few years, but German champions Bayern Munich won the race to sign him from Ajax last summer. The Dutchman is at his best when sitting deep and bossing games by spraying passes around, but he's also got a rocket long-range shot!

IS HE THE NEXT... TONI KROOS?

Kroos is one of the best passers in Europe, and Gravenberch has the potential to be just as good! He could be pulling strings in Bayern's midfield for ages – just like Kroos did before moving to Real Madrid!

ERATION!

MATCH takes a look at some of the other young pretenders ready to take over the footy world in the next few years...

GONCALO INACIO

Position: Centre-back

Age: 21 ★ Club: Sporting

Classy central defender Inacio broke into Portuguese giants Sporting's first team in 2020-21 and became a regular as the club won their first league title in 19 years! Despite his age he's ice cold under pressure, and is just as good at snuffing out attacks as he is at playing out from defence with his classy left foot!

IS HE THE NEXT... RUBEN DIAS?

Inacio is like a left-footed version of the Man. City defender, combining rock-solid defending with slick ability on the ball. Portugal's defence will be safe in the future with these two at the heart of it!

FABIO CARVALHO

Position: Att. midfielder/winger

Age: 20 ★ Club: Liverpool

Carvalho grabbed ten goals and eight assists to fire Fulham to the Championship title and Premier League promotion in 2021-22, earning him a dream £7.7m move to Liverpool! Reds boss Jurgen Klopp rates him for his flair, creativity and versatility – he rocked the Championship as a No.10, but can also play deeper or out wide!

IS HE THE NEXT... PHILIPPE COUTINHO?

Coutinho is also effective in a few different positions, and he used to rock Anfield with his dribbling ability and eye for spectacular goals and assists! Carvalho would love to follow in the Brazilian's footsteps!

RAYAN CHERKI

Position: Winger

Age: 19 ★ Club: Lyon

Although he's still a teenager, Cherki has already played well over 50 games for Lyon in all competitions, and has a massive year ahead of him in 2023! We love watching him because he's got so much flair and skill, and is capable of making defenders look silly - with more goals and assists he'll be world class!

IS HE THE NEXT... RIYAD MAHREZ?

Watching Cherki cutting in from the right, terrorising full-backs and unleashing left-footed shots is just like watching Mahrez! The Lyon man has Algerian parents too, so could even join Riyad in the national team!

GOAL KING #2
LEWANDOWSKI

There's a reason why the BARCELONA ace is nicknamed "Lewan-goalski" – the POLAND forward was just born to score goals! After dominating German football for a decade, he's now ready to tear it up in Spain!

GOALSCORING GAME

✓ Now into his 30s, Lewy has to rely on his brain more than his pace. Luckily for him, he can still outthink any defender to find space in the box!

✓ The ex-Bayern Munich striker's first touch is key to scoring goals. He's a master at creating space for a shot or nailing one in first time!

✓ Left foot, right foot, headers - it doesn't matter! If Lewandowski gets a sight of goal inside the box, he nearly always rips the back of the net!

BEST SEASON

Lewandowski needed a new trophy cabinet after his insane 2019-20 campaign! He fired Bayern to the treble of Champions League, Bundesliga and the German Cup - winning the Golden Boot in each comp - and picked up his first FIFA Best Player award after ending the campaign with 55 goals in total. Wow!

LAST SEASON

Over the last few seasons Lewandowski has gone from being a world-class striker to one of the deadliest goal machines of all time! He netted 50 goals in all comps in 2021-22 to pick up his second European Golden Shoe in a row and fifth straight Bundesliga Golden Boot on the way to his tenth league-winners' medal in Germany!

GREATEST GOAL

Bayern Munich	5	1	Wolfsburg

September 22 2015 Lewy scored a stunning five goals in just nine minutes after coming on as a sub in this game, but the fifth was the pick of the bunch – he ripped the net with an unstoppable scissor-kick!

STAT PACK

1 With over 70 goals in less than 140 caps, he is No.1 on Poland's all-time scoring list!

£42.5M Barca paid over £40m for Lewy, making the Pole one of the most expensive players over 30 ever!

344 He left Bayern Munich as their second-highest scorer of all time with 344 goals!

41 In 2020-21 he broke the record for goals scored in a single Bundesliga season!

WHAT'S NEXT?

The Poland hitman stunned Bayern by leaving them last summer, and now has his sights on banging in goals for Barcelona! The La Liga giants need a new goal hero to take them back to the top of La Liga and the Champions League after the departures of Lionel Messi and Luis Suarez in recent years, and Lewy is ready to step up!

Stats correct up to start of the 2022-23 season.

MATCH! 35

BIG MATCH QUIZ!

How many of these epic Euro league teasers can you get right?

NAME THE TEAM!

Name the players who lined up for Real Madrid in the 2022 Spanish Super Cup final!

1. BELGIUM ★ GOALKEEPER

2. AUSTRIA ★ CENTRE-BACK

3. GERMANY ★ MIDFIELDER

4. BRAZIL ★ CENTRE-BACK

5. BRAZIL ★ MIDFIELDER

6. FRANCE ★ STRIKER

7. SPAIN ★ RIGHT-BACK

8. FRANCE ★ LEFT-BACK

BRAZIL ★ WINGER
RODRYGO

9. BRAZIL ★ WINGER

10. CROATIA ★ MIDFIELDER

BABY FACE

Name the superstar in this snap from before they were famous!

MATCH! WINNER!

Who scored the winner in Bayern's 3–2 win over Dortmund in December 2021?

LEGENDARY

Which massive clubs did these footy legends win league titles with?

1. Victor Valdes

2. Javier Zanetti

3. Alessandro Del Piero

4. Roberto Carlos

5. Paolo Maldini

6. Oliver Kahn

CROSSWORD

Use the clues to fill in our awesome Euro leagues crossword!

ACROSS

3. Current Premier League team ex-France midfielder Etienne Capoue used to play for! (9)

6. Atletico Madrid's eccentric Argentine manager! (5,7)

8. Team that won the 2020-21 Ligue 1 title! (5)

10. The only French side ever to have lifted the European Cup! (9)

13. French club Monaco's three-letter initials! (3)

16. Huge Portuguese club Man. United superstar Bruno Fernandes used to play for! (8)

17. La Liga's all-time top goalscorer! (6,5)

18. The Spanish city where you'll find Real Betis! (7)

19. The number of teams that compete in the German Bundesliga every year! (8)

DOWN

1. The 2021-22 Bundesliga top goalscorer! (6,11)

2. The name of Bayern Munich's epic stadium! (7,5)

4. Villarreal's cool sea-related nickname! (3,6,9)

5. Team Barcelona signed Frenkie de Jong from! (4)

7. Turkish side Mesut Ozil left Arsenal to join! (10)

9. Shirt number that Brazil's Neymar wears for PSG! (3)

11. Famous ground of Inter and AC Milan! (3,4)

12. Barcelona manager Xavi's last name! (9)

14. Borussia Dortmund's big local rivals! (7)

15. Main colour of Bayer Leverkusen's away kit in 2021-22! (5)

17. French team wonderkid Rayan Cherki plays for! (4)

DESIGN 3 PREM BALLS!

MATCH wants you to design three Premier League footballs for the 2023-24 season! We need one for the first stage of the season, one for the winter months and one for the business end of the campaign!

GET DOODLING RIGHT NOW!

Check out some of these real footballs for inspiration!

BALL 1 AUGUST TO OCTOBER

BALL 2 NOVEMBER TO FEBRUARY

Remember, the winter ball needs to be mega bright so that it stands out in bad weather!

BALL 3 MARCH TO MAY

SEND IT IN!

Send your awesome designs into MATCH and we'll feature our favourites in the magazine and on our epic social media channels!

@ Email: match.magazine@kelsey.co.uk

f facebook.com/matchmagazine

twitter.com/matchmagazine

instagram.com/matchmagofficial

Try to get the MATCH logo somewhere on each footy!

WORLD CUP DREAM TEAM!

There's gonna be loads of world-class players on show at QATAR 2022 – now imagine that you had the chance to put together an unreal line-up including whoever you wanted! Pick your WC dream team and send it in to MATCH – we'll feature the best ones in our magazine!

WORLD CUP DREAM TEAM
GOALKEEPERS!

THIBAUT COURTOIS
BELGIUM

If anybody had any doubts about whether Courtois is one of the best goalkeepers in the world, they should watch the 2022 Champions League final! Real Madrid would have definitely lost to Liverpool if it wasn't for the big Belgian between the sticks, and he's more than capable of dragging his country to glory too!

HUGO LLORIS
FRANCE

Lloris is more than a world-class goalkeeper, he's also an inspirational leader. The Tottenham star wore the captain's armband as France lifted the World Cup in 2018, and has led his country out more than any other player in French history! He could break his country's caps record in Qatar too!

EMILIANO MARTINEZ
ARGENTINA

In 2021 Argentina won the Copa America – their first trophy in almost 30 years – but they couldn't have done it without Martinez. The Aston Villa ace was named the tournament's best GK after keeping four clean sheets on the way to the trophy and starring in the penalty shootout win over Colombia!

GUILLERMO OCHOA
MEXICO

Ochoa might not be a household name in Europe, but in Mexico he's a legend for his sick World Cup displays! The epic acrobat made tons of saves in both the 2014 and 2018 tournaments, so if you want a player that'll rise to the big occasion then he's the man for you!

ALISSON
BRAZIL

When it comes to goalkeepers, no WC manager is spoilt for choice like Brazil boss Tite! With Alisson and Ederson, he hasn't just got two of the best goalies in the Prem, but two of the very best on the planet! Alisson got the gloves in qualifying and should be No.1 in Qatar!

BEST OF THE REST!
CHECK OUT THESE OTHER SUPERSTARS!

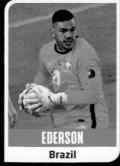
MANUEL NEUER
Germany

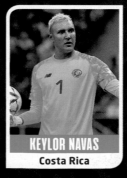
EDERSON
Brazil

KEYLOR NAVAS
Costa Rica

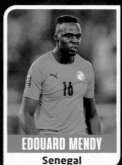
EDOUARD MENDY
Senegal

NOW PICK YOUR WORLD CUP 2022 DREAM TEAM GOALKEEPERS!

TURN TO PAGE 52

WORLD CUP DREAM TEAM
CENTRE-BACKS!

RAPHAEL VARANE
FRANCE
Varane has been one of the best defenders in the world for ages, and he's got the medals to prove it! With four Champions Leagues, a World Cup and tons of other trophies, he's one of the most successful players on the planet, and will be one of the first names on Didier Deschamps' teamsheet!

JOSE GIMENEZ
URUGUAY
Gimenez and his experienced team-mate Diego Godin know every single defensive trick in the book from their days playing together for Uruguay and Atletico Madrid, so strikers absolutely hate playing against the tough duo!

HARRY MAGUIRE
ENGLAND
Maguire might not be the most popular player with Man. United fans, but he is like a different player when he pulls on an England shirt! He's class at bringing the ball out and wins everything in the air for The Three Lions - that's why he was one of the stars of Russia 2018!

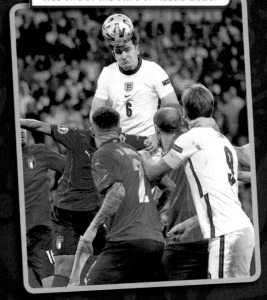

MARQUINHOS
BRAZIL
If you were building the perfect centre-back, he'd probably look a lot like Marquinhos. He's an athletic and intelligent defender with the passing range of a central midfielder, plus he captains both PSG and Brazil! His partnership with Eder Militao is rock solid too - the pair didn't concede a single goal when they played together in World Cup qualifying!

VIRGIL VAN DIJK
NETHERLANDS
We reckon every manager in the world would pick Van Dijk if they had the chance - he's unbelievably good! The Liverpool man is ice cool under pressure, reads opponents' attacks like a book and can match anybody in a race or an arm-wrestle! On top of all that, he's the Dutch captain too!

BEST OF THE REST!
CHECK OUT THESE OTHER SUPERSTARS!

RUBEN DIAS
Portugal

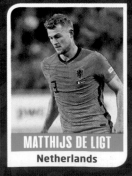
THIAGO SILVA
Brazil

MATTHIJS DE LIGT
Netherlands

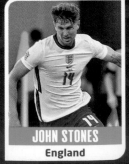
SIMON KJAER
Denmark

JOHN STONES
England

AYMERIC LAPORTE

SPAIN

Laporte was actually born in France, and even played for the French youth teams, but qualified to play for Spain after coming through the ranks at Athletic Bilbao. We can't believe that he never got a cap for Les Bleus, especially after seeing the classy defender boss the Spanish back-line at Euro 2020!

KALIDOU KOULIBALY

SENEGAL

The Senegal skipper will go to Qatar with tons of confidence after leading his country to the AFCON trophy at the start of 2022! The Chelsea star has absolutely everything - as well as being a legendary leader, Koulibaly is so quick, strong and tough that he can keep any opposition attacker in his back pocket!

CRISTIAN ROMERO

ARGENTINA

The ex-Atalanta centre-back has been one of Tottenham's smartest signings for ages, and was a key man in Argentina's Copa America-winning defence too. He'll throw his body in the way of absolutely anything to help his side keep a clean sheet!

NAYEF AGUERD

MOROCCO

Aguerd was one of the most expensive players in West Ham's history when he arrived in East London last summer. He started out as an attacking midfielder before switching to centre-back, so he's got classy passing skills combined with being a rock-solid defender!

JOSKO GVARDIOL

CROATIA

Gvardiol doesn't turn 21 until after the World Cup is over, but he's already one of the most-wanted defenders in Europe! He had a wicked season after joining RB Leipzig in 2021 to prove that he's a star of club football - now he's ready to show it in a Croatia shirt too!

BEN DAVIES
Wales

EDER MILITAO
Brazil

PRESNEL KIMPEMBE
France

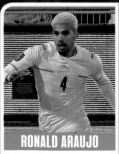

RONALD ARAUJO
Uruguay

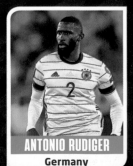

ANTONIO RUDIGER
Germany

NOW PICK YOUR WORLD CUP 2022 DREAM TEAM CENTRE-BACKS!

TURN TO PAGE 52

WORLD CUP DREAM TEAM
FULL-BACKS!

KYLE WALKER

ENGLAND

Gareth Southgate's options at right-back are totally insane, with Walker competing with Reece James, Trent Alexander-Arnold and Kieran Trippier! The England boss loves the Man. City man because of his experience, epic recovery skills and, most importantly, his electric pace. He makes The Three Lions' back-line so solid!

DAVID RAUM

GERMANY

Left-back has been a problem position for Germany for ages, but not anymore. Raum was one of the stars of the Bundesliga in 2021-22, picking up 11 assists for Hoffenheim, before nailing his place in the German starting line-up during the UEFA Nations League!

ALPHONSO DAVIES

CANADA

The Bayern Munich star might be the quickest player on the planet right now! Although he's awesome at using his pace to end opposition attacks, Canada like using his skill and dribbling ability at the other end of the pitch. He could definitely be one of the stars of Qatar!

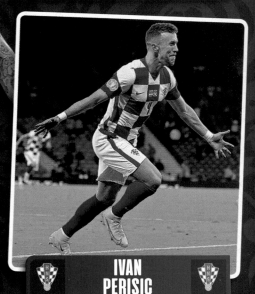

JOAKIM MAEHLE

DENMARK

With five goals and three assists, Maehle was Denmark's best attacker during World Cup qualifying. The versatile star can play on either flank, but usually does his best work from the left, where he can cut onto his right foot and take shots or whip in crosses!

IVAN PERISIC

CROATIA

Perisic might line up on the left wing of Croatia's attack, but he's spent the last couple of years playing as a wing-back in club football. He's a seriously dangerous attacker because he's just as good at whipping in crosses as he is at getting on the end of them!

BEST OF THE REST!
CHECK OUT THESE OTHER SUPERSTARS!

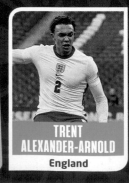

TRENT ALEXANDER-ARNOLD
England

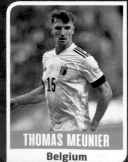

THOMAS MEUNIER
Belgium

DANI CARVAJAL
Spain

BENJAMIN PAVARD
France

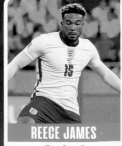

REECE JAMES
England

JOAO CANCELO

PORTUGAL

The Man. City man can play on the right or left side of defence, but he's so good at passing and tackling that he could probably do a job in central midfield too! He picked up seven assists in last season's Premier League-winning season, and will add serious creativity to Portugal's side!

CESAR AZPILICUETA

SPAIN

These days, a lot of full-backs are known for their attacking ability, but Azpilicueta is just a straightforward, rock-solid defender! He's got tons of experience, can play anywhere along the back-line and is capable of keeping even the best attackers quiet!

FILIP KOSTIC

SERBIA

Kostic was named Player of the Tournament as Eintracht Frankfurt won last season's Europa League – his performances from wing-back were simply incredible! He picks up tons of assists because he's one of the best crossers in Europe, so strikers absolutely love playing with him!

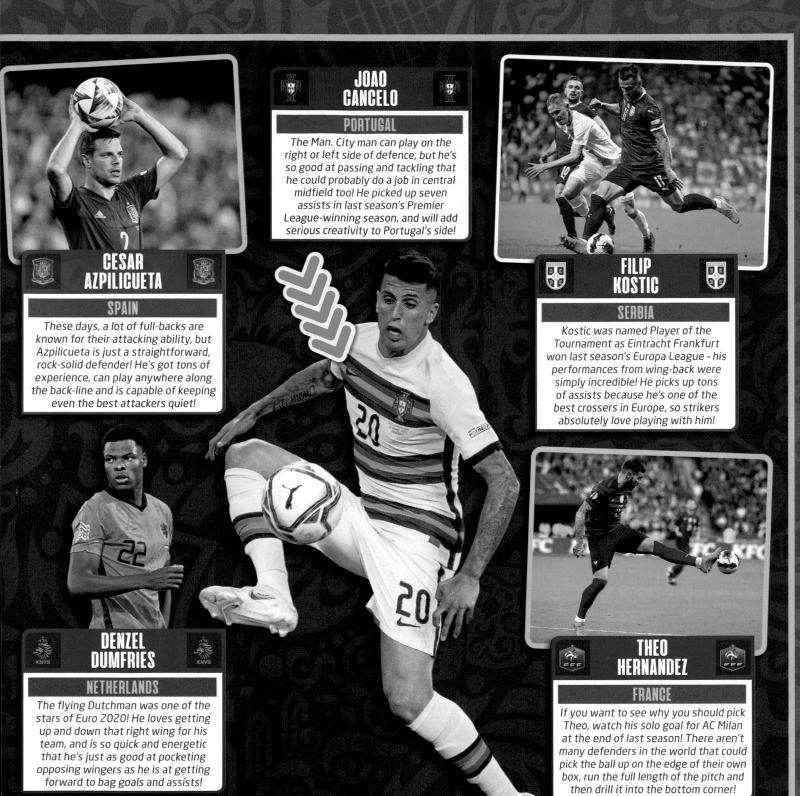

DENZEL DUMFRIES

NETHERLANDS

The flying Dutchman was one of the stars of Euro 2020! He loves getting up and down that right wing for his team, and is so quick and energetic that he's just as good at pocketing opposing wingers as he is at getting forward to bag goals and assists!

THEO HERNANDEZ

FRANCE

If you want to see why you should pick Theo, watch his solo goal for AC Milan at the end of last season! There aren't many defenders in the world that could pick the ball up on the edge of their own box, run the full length of the pitch and then drill it into the bottom corner!

ACHRAF HAKIMI
Morocco

FERLAND MENDY
France

LUKE SHAW
England

JORDI ALBA
Spain

MATTY CASH
Poland

NOW PICK YOUR WORLD CUP 2022 DREAM TEAM FULL-BACKS!

TURN TO PAGE 52

WORLD CUP DREAM TEAM
MIDFIELDERS!

KEVIN DE BRUYNE
BELGIUM

As long as De Bruyne is on the pitch, Belgium have a chance of going all the way in Qatar. The Man. City superstar is capable of winning games all by himself, because he can score or create a goal with either foot from anywhere!

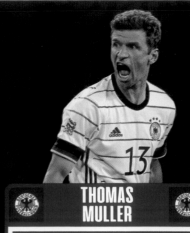

THOMAS MULLER
GERMANY

Muller has the chance to become a legend in Qatar! No current player has scored more WC goals than him, and he only needs one more to become the top-scoring midfielder in WC history! With two assists, he can match the all-time assists record too!

SERGIO BUSQUETS
SPAIN

Now aged 34, this could be Busquets' last World Cup. He lifted the trophy in 2010, and is just as important to Spain now as he was then. The Barca legend isn't quick or strong, but that doesn't matter because he's so intelligent and never gives the ball away!

JUDE BELLINGHAM
ENGLAND

The all-action midfielder has the potential to be one of the best players on the planet, and this could be the World Cup where he shows it! He's basically got everything you could want in a midfielder - quality passing, tons of skill and solid tackling, plus he's an absolute beast who can run all day!

CHRISTIAN ERIKSEN
DENMARK

After the horrendous scenes at Euro 2020, it's a miracle that Eriksen is still playing at all. But since the playmaker's comeback, he's been playing some of the best footy of his career! As well as getting tons of assists with his creativity and set-piece delivery, he's also one of Denmark's all-time top scorers!

BEST OF THE REST!
CHECK OUT THESE OTHER SUPERSTARS!

FRENKIE DE JONG
Netherlands

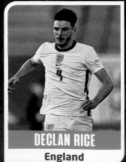

DECLAN RICE
England

DUSAN TADIC
Serbia

PAUL POGBA
France

GRANIT XHAKA
Switzerland

CASEMIRO

BRAZIL

CDM is another position where Brazil have unreal strength in depth – as well as Liverpool's midfield boss Fabinho, they've also got a five-time Champions League winner in Casemiro! The rock-solid shielder is an absolute master at winning the ball back, and allows team-mates like Neymar to shine in attack!

LUKA MODRIC

CROATIA

In 2018, Modric almost got his hands on the World Cup trophy as Croatia lost to France in the final. They'd have never got that far without their super skipper, though – Luka totally bosses games with his elite-level passing, dribbling and creativity, and will still be going strong in Qatar at the age of 37!

FEDE VALVERDE

URUGUAY

Valverde is one of the most versatile players around, so you could basically pick him wherever you like in your dream team! The Real Madrid ace usually starts in central midfield for Uruguay, but he's just as comfortable playing on the wing, as a No.10 or a second striker because he's got tons of skill and energy!

JOSHUA KIMMICH

GERMANY

Kimmich started his career at right-back – and could still do a top job there now – but has played in midfield for the last few seasons and has absolutely bossed it! In the Bundesliga he gets ten assists a year at least thanks to his unreal passing, but he's still got the tackling ability of a world-class full-back!

N'GOLO KANTE

FRANCE

If you want a disciplined midfielder who will run all day, you've got to pick Kante. The Chelsea star has been so consistent for so long that people forget just how good he is – he was vital to France's World Cup victory in 2018, and will be key in Qatar too!

BRUNO FERNANDES
Portugal

PEDRI
Spain

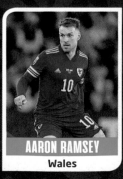

AARON RAMSEY
Wales

RODRI
Spain

FABINHO
Brazil

NOW PICK YOUR WORLD CUP 2022 DREAM MIDFIELDERS!

TURN TO PAGE 52

WORLD CUP DREAM TEAM
WINGERS!

 KYLIAN MBAPPE

FRANCE

Mbappe absolutely tore up Russia 2018, scoring four goals and winning the Young Player of the Tournament to fire France to the trophy! Back then he was still a teenager, but now he's matured into one of the best players in the world. When the pacy forward gets going, he's unstoppable!

BERNARDO SILVA

PORTUGAL

The silky superstar is just as good out wide as he is in the centre of midfield. He can carve defences open with his sweet left foot, or tie them in knots with his slick dribbling ability! With Cristiano Ronaldo getting on, Bernardo will be Portugal's main man!

CHRISTIAN PULISIC

USA

The sizzling forward will only be 24 in Qatar, but some USA fans already reckon he might be the country's biggest talent ever! He'll be the main man for his team at the finals, making things happen with his quick feet, clever movement and fearless flair!

VINICIUS JUNIOR

BRAZIL

There's tons of pressure on Neymar to deliver Brazil's sixth World Cup in 2022, so he'll be buzzing to have a talent like Vini alongside him! He was one of the stars of the season as Real Madrid lifted their 14th Champions League, not only bagging the winner in the final but also destroying defenders along the way!

GARETH BALE

WALES

It's crazy to think that before Bale came onto the scene, Wales hadn't played at a major tournament for ages - now they're at a first World Cup since 1958! The wing wizard always delivers for them when they need him - he only needs a sight of goal to unleash a stunner with his lethal left foot!

BEST OF THE REST!
CHECK OUT THESE OTHER SUPERSTARS!

RAHEEM STERLING
England

RAFAEL LEAO
Portugal

LEROY SANE
Germany

BRENNAN JOHNSON
Wales

EDEN HAZARD
Belgium

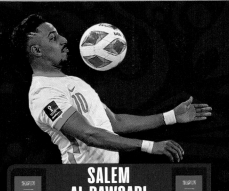

  ## LIONEL MESSI

ARGENTINA

Make the most of watching Messi in the World Cup, because it will probably be his last. He's tried to win the trophy four times before, but this time he's going with international silverware already in his trophy cabinet! After winning the 2021 Copa America and Finalissima, can Leo get his hands on the trophy he wants the most?

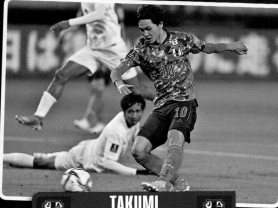

SALEM AL DAWSARI

SAUDI ARABIA

If you want your dream team to play with flair, then get Al Dawsari involved – he's got a habit of scoring worldies out of nowhere! The Saudi's star man is just as capable of nailing a bicycle kick as he is of dribbling the length of the pitch and dinking it over the keeper!

 ## TAKUMI MINAMINO

JAPAN

Only two Asian players scored more times than Minamino in World Cup qualifying as he fired Japan to Qatar with ten goals! Full-backs hate playing against him because he's rapid and never stops running, and when he gets into the area he's a clinical finisher!

SADIO MANE

SENEGAL

Mane has already tasted international glory in 2022 after winning the AFCON title in February! As well as bagging three goals and two assists in Senegal's epic victory, the ex-Liverpool man also buried the decisive penalty in the final shootout! He's ice-cool under pressure!

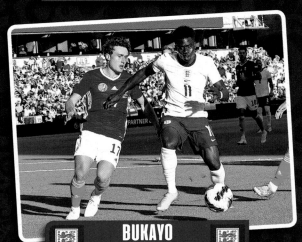

BUKAYO SAKA

ENGLAND

Saka is going to be a star for England and Arsenal for years! As well as being rapid, the 21-year-old has tons of tricks in his locker, and will go to Qatar full of confidence after scoring 12 goals in the 2021-22 season. You can also pick him as a left wing-back in your dream team!

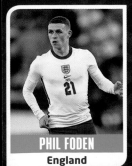

PHIL FODEN
England

NEYMAR
Brazil

SON HEUNG-MIN
South Korea

ANSU FATI
Spain

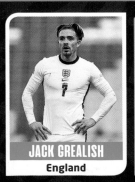

JACK GREALISH
England

NOW PICK YOUR WORLD CUP DREAM TEAM WINGERS!

TURN TO PAGE 52

WORLD CUP DREAM TEAM
STRIKERS!

KARIM BENZEMA
FRANCE

Benzema's a terrifying opponent for defenders because he only needs a glimpse of goal to find the back of the net! He has been in the form of his life in 2022 and, after playing a starring role in Real Madrid's run to the Champions League trophy, he'd love to add a World Cup medal!

DARWIN NUNEZ
URUGUAY

Luis Suarez and Edinson Cavani have led Uruguay's attack for years, but now there's a new superstar in town! Liverpool splashed out mega cash for Nunez after he ran their defence ragged in the Champions League playing for Benfica, and he'll be even better by the time the World Cup starts!

ROBERT LEWANDOWSKI
POLAND

The Barcelona hitman might be well into his 30s now, but he's still one of the very best goalscorers on the planet! He fired Poland to Qatar with nine goals in qualifying, and during the last three seasons he's scored 150 club goals - more than any other player in Europe's top five leagues!

ALMOEZ ALI
QATAR

All the Qatar players will be hoping to make a name for themselves at their first-ever World Cup, and none more so than Ali. He was the top goalscorer and best player when the team won the Asian Cup in 2019, and would love to bring that form to the world stage!

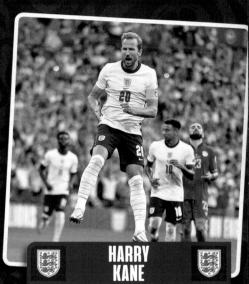

HARRY KANE
ENGLAND

Kane is a special striker because not only is he a ruthless finisher with his head or either foot, he's also able to drop deep and spray around unreal passes - that's why he bags so many assists! The 2018 World Cup Golden Boot winner is absolutely desperate to fire England to the World Cup!

BEST OF THE REST!
CHECK OUT THESE OTHER SUPERSTARS!

MEMPHIS DEPAY
Netherlands

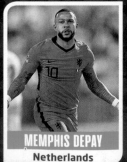
LAUTARO MARTINEZ
Argentina

ANTOINE GRIEZMANN
France

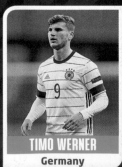
TIMO WERNER
Germany

ROMELU LUKAKU
Belgium

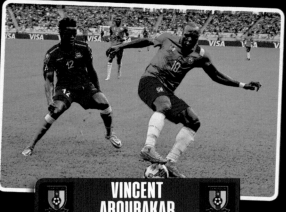

CRISTIANO RONALDO

PORTUGAL

A World Cup medal is basically the only thing missing from Ronaldo's trophy cabinet, but he'll be going all out to change that! He only needs one goal in Qatar to become the first player in history to score at five different World Cup tournaments. Legend!

VINCENT ABOUBAKAR

CAMEROON

At the start of 2022, Aboubakar almost fired Cameroon to AFCON glory with eight goals! The Al Nassr man was the highest scorer in the tournament for almost 50 years, and if he takes that form to Qatar he could be a real threat. He proper bullies defenders!

DUSAN VLAHOVIC

SERBIA

There's a reason why Juventus splashed out big money on Vlahovic in 2022 - he's got the potential to be one of the best No.9s in the world! He's got the pace and strength to dominate defenders, but his left foot is absolutely explosive - his shots can bust through the net!

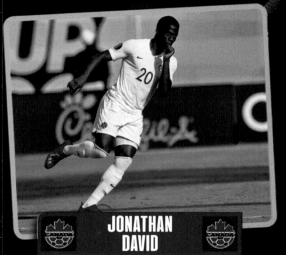

JONATHAN DAVID

CANADA

David formed an absolutely deadly strike partnership with Cyle Larin to fire Canada to Qatar, scoring 22 times between them! The Lille forward is only 22 but he's already an absolutely clinical finisher, and will be desperate to make Canada's first World Cup in 36 years a memorable one!

MEHDI TAREMI

IRAN

Iran are blessed with two dangerous strikers in the form of Leverkusen's Sardar Azmoun and Porto's Taremi! The tall forward has been tearing up the Portuguese league ever since he arrived in 2019, bagging 49 goals and 25 assists in his first three years!

ALEKSANDAR MITROVIC
Serbia

RAUL JIMENEZ
Mexico

DIOGO JOTA
Portugal

LUIS SUAREZ
Uruguay

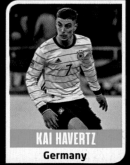

KAI HAVERTZ
Germany

NOW PICK YOUR WORLD CUP 2022 DREAM TEAM STRIKERS!

TURN OVER NOW...

MY WORLD CUP DREAM TEAM!

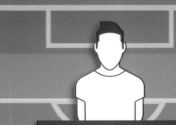

GOALKEEPER

RIGHT-BACK

CENTRE-BACK

CENTRE-BACK

LEFT-BACK

WINGER

MIDFIELDER

MIDFIELDER

WINGER

STRIKER

STRIKER

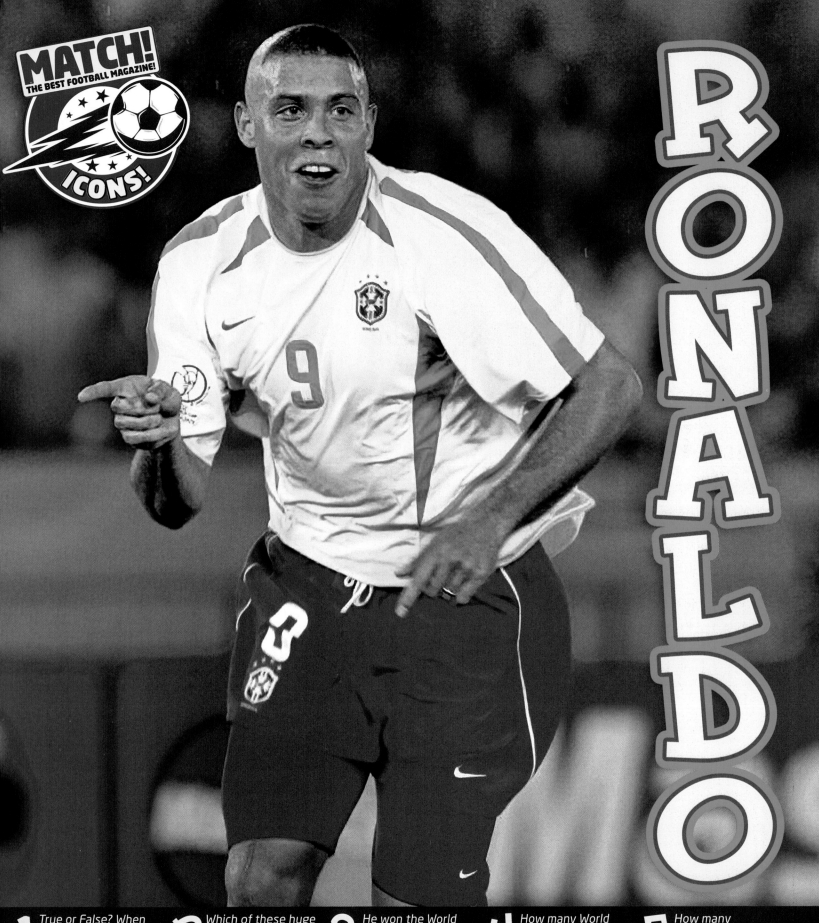

MATCH!
THE BEST FOOTBALL MAGAZINE!
ICONS!

RONALDO

1 True or False? When he first started playing for Brazil in the 1990s, he was actually known as "Ronaldinho"!

2 Which of these huge clubs did he never play for - Barcelona, Inter, PSV, Juventus, Real Madrid or AC Milan?

3 He won the World Cup Golden Boot with eight goals at which tournament - 1998, 2002 or 2006?

4 How many World Cup goals did "O Fenomeno" score in total during his career - six, nine, 11, 13 or 15?

5 How many international caps did the lethal Brazil striker win overall - more or less than 100?

ANSWERS ON PAGE 94 ➜

BIG MATCH QUIZ!

How many of these mind-boggling EFL teasers can you get right?

SOCCER SCRAMBLE!

Can you re-arrange these letters to find four Championship stars?

HISRC WLOKCLI

JNDOAR SRDOHE

KNLAAR TRGNA

SAAREDN EIWNANM

NAME THE CLUB!

Which massive Championship club's recent record is this?

Year	Position
2022	7TH
2021	10TH
2020	17TH
2019	7TH
2018	5TH

BOGUS BADGE!

Name the EFL club that this badge belongs to!

HIGHER OR LOWER?

Billy Sharp scored 14 league goals in 2021-22! How did these other ballers compare?

	HIGHER	LOWER
1. Ben Brereton Diaz	✓	✓
2. Elijah Adebayo	✓	✓
3. Benik Afobe	✓	✓
4. Chris Martin	✓	✓
5. Viktor Gyokeres	✓	✓

ACE ACTIVITY

WORDSEARCH

Barnsley	Exeter	Luton	Northampton	Reading	Sutton
Birmingham	Forest Green	Mansfield	Oxford	Rotherham	Swindon
Blackpool	Hartlepool	Middlesbrough	Peterborough	Salford	Tranmere
Bolton	Hull	Millwall	Port Vale	Stoke	Wigan
Charlton	Ipswich	MK Dons	Portsmouth	Sunderland	Wycombe

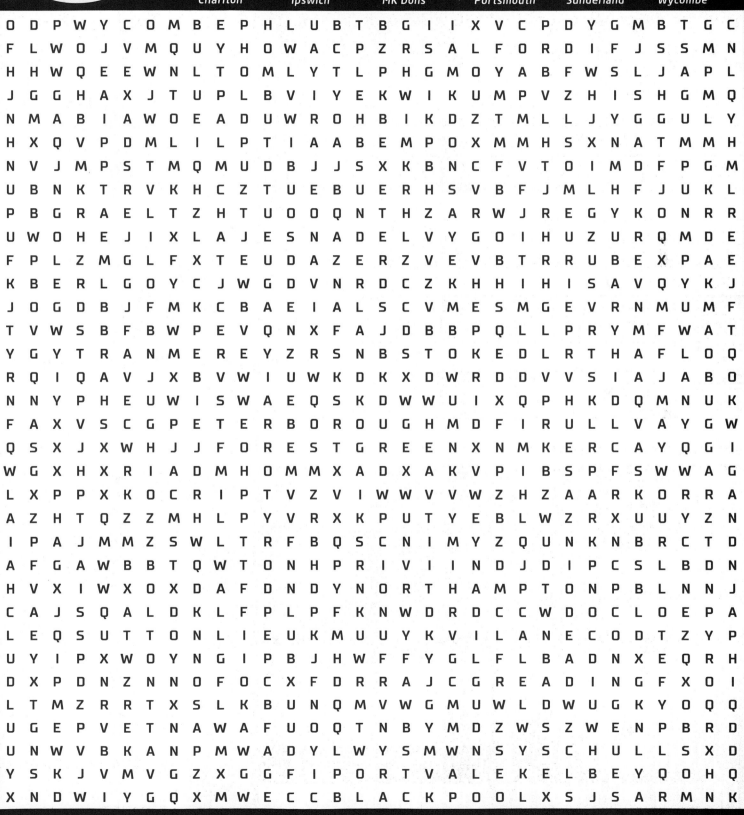

```
O D P W Y C O M B E P H L U B T B G I I X V C P D Y G M B T G C
F L W O J V M Q U Y H O W A C P Z R S A L F O R D I F J S S M N
H H W Q E E W N L T O M L Y T L P H G M O Y A B F W S L J A P L
J G G H A X J T U P L B V I Y E K W I K U M P V Z H I S H G M Q
N M A B I A W O E A D U W R O H B I K D Z T M L L J Y G G U L Y
H X Q V P D M L I L P T I A A B E M P O X M M H S X N A T M M H
N V J M P S T M Q M U D B J J S X K B N C F V T O I M D F P G M
U B N K T R V K H C Z T U E B U E R H S V B F J M L H F J U K L
P B G R A E L T Z H T U O O Q N T H Z A R W J R E G Y K O N R R
U W O H E J I X L A J E S N A D E L V Y G O I H U Z U R Q M D E
F P L Z M G L F X T E U D A Z E R Z V E V B T R R U B E X P A E
K B E R L G O Y C J W G D V N R D C Z K H H I H I S A V Q Y K J
J O G D B J F M K C B A E I A L S C V M E S M G E V R N M U M F
T V W S B F B W P E V Q N X F A J D B B P Q L L P R Y M F W A T
Y G Y T R A N M E R E Y Z R S N B S T O K E D L R T H A F L O Q
R Q I Q A V J X B V W I U W K D K X D W R D D V V S I A J A B O
N N Y P H E U W I S W A E Q S K D W W U I X Q P H K D Q M N U K
F A X V S C G P E T E R B O R O U G H M D F I R U L L V A Y G W
Q S X J X W H J J F O R E S T G R E E N X N M K E R C A Y Q G I
W G X H X R I A D M H O M M X A D X A K V P I B S P F S W W A G
L X P P X K O C R I P T V Z V I W V W Z H Z A A R K O R R A
A Z H T Q Z Z M H L P Y V R X K P U T Y E B L W Z R X U U Y Z N
I P A J M M Z S W L T R F B Q S C N I M Y Z Q U N K N B R C T D
A F G A W B B T Q W T O N H P R I V I I N D J D I P C S L B D N
H V X I W X O X D A F D N D Y N O R T H A M P T O N P B L N N J
C A J S Q A L D K L F P L P F K N W D R D C C W D O C L O E P A
L E Q S U T T O N L I E U K M U U Y K V I L A N E C O D T Z Y P
U Y I P X W O Y N G I P B J H W F F Y G L F L B A D N X E Q R D
D X P D N Z N N O F O C X F D R R A J C G R E A D I N G F X O I
L T M Z R R T X S L K B U N Q M V W G M U W L D W U G K Y O Q Q
U G E P V E T N A W A F U O Q T N B Y M D Z W S Z W E N P B R D
U N W V B K A N P M W A D Y L W Y S M W N S Y S C H U L L S X D
Y S K J V M V G Z X G G F I P O R T V A L E K E L B E Y Q O H Q
X N D W I Y G Q X M W E C C B L A C K P O O L X S J S A R M N K
```

SNAPPED!
BEST OF 2022!

Close up!

The TV viewers could see what Kate Longhurst had for breakfast!

Short shorts!

Or is that just a giant nappy?

Funny fan!

We're not sure why this Cameroon supporter was so serious?

Mohawk mess!

Arturo Vidal was in tears because someone ruffled his Mohawk!

Footy fail!

Vydra and Soucek took their 'head-to-head' way too literally. LOL!

Barca band!

Barcelona Femeni's Asisat Oshoala always 'beats' her opponents! Ba dum tish...

Hammer hold!

Yeah, good luck getting out of that headlock!

JUST TAP OUT ALREADY!

Boca breakdancer!

JLINGZ, EAT YOUR HEART OUT!

That should be saved for the dance floor not the football pitch, mate!

Grumpy Guardiola!

I WON'T TAKE NO FOR AN ANSWER!

MATCH reckons Trent must have turned down a move to Man. City!

Lift off!

THE MATCH ANNUAL IS OUT!

Has Hughes got rockets in his studs?

WHERE YOU GOING, BRO?

Mad Marcelo!

Marcelo dressed up all of Madrid's statues in his side's colours!

IT'S MY MASTERPIECE, MATCH!

Boss banter!

3-1! HA-HA!

When you remind your mate what happened last time on FIFA!

GOAL KING #3
BENZEMA

REAL MADRID and **FRANCE** superstar **KARIM BENZEMA** was arguably the best player in the world during 2022, inspiring his club to both the Champions League and La Liga trophies!

GOALSCORING GAME

✓ Benzema is one of the smartest strikers around! His footy brain and movement are elite, so he's always in the right place at the right time!

✓ He's so clinical that he only needs a glimpse of goal to score - as he proved with his 17-minute hat-trick against PSG in the Champions League!

✓ The Frenchman isn't just deadly with his feet - his hat-trick against Chelsea featured two of the best headers you'll ever see. Total legend!

FACTPACK!
Club: *Real Madrid*
Country: *France*
Age: *34*
Height: *6ft 1in*
Top Skill: *World-class movement!*

BREAKTHROUGH SEASON

Back in 2007-08, Benzema made a name for himself as one of the hottest young talents in Europe! French club Lyon were on their way to a seventh title in a row, with a 20-year-old striker topping the Ligue 1 scoring charts! He hit 31 goals in all competitions, including a sick finish against Man. United in the Champions League!

LAST SEASON

Benzema has got better and better ever since Cristiano Ronaldo left Real Madrid in 2018, and the Frenchman was in the form of his life in 2021-22! As well as ending the campaign as La Liga's top scorer as Madrid lifted the title, he inspired them to three comeback wins in a row against PSG, Chelsea and Man. City on the way to the Champions League trophy!

STAT PACK

44 In 2021-22, Benzema scored 44 goals in just 46 games in all comps!

323 He ended the season by going joint-second with Raul on Real Madrid's all-time top scorers list!

10 Ten of his 15 Champions League goals last season came in the knockout rounds!

5 He didn't play for France for six years, yet he's still his country's fifth-highest goalscorer in history!

GREATEST GOAL

Lyon	1	1	Man. United

February 20, 2008 This goal showed Benzema at his clinical and instinctive best - he only needed three touches to make Man. United legends Rio Ferdinand and Nemanja Vidic look like League Two defenders!

WHAT'S NEXT?

Benzema was left out when France won the 2018 World Cup, so he'd love to get his hands on the trophy this time around. After that, he's got Cristiano Ronaldo's record of 450 Real Madrid goals in his sights - although it'll take him a few years to get there!

FIFA TIPS....
FROM THE PROS!

MATCH has spoken to tons of professional ePremier League finalists to get their most important FIFA tips for you! Check this awesome advice out...

OLLE ARBIN

OLLE SAYS: "If you want to improve on Weekend League, it's very important to take pauses. You can't play 30 games in a row – it's not good for your brain or yourself! You should also play players that are better than you as you will learn new things. And definitely learn the directional bridge! It gives you a huge speed boost and can beat a one-v-one situation very easily!"

DIOGO MENDES

DIOGO SAYS: "If you're playing Weekend League, my main tip is when you lose a game, don't go straight into another one! When you go straight into another game, you're still going to be mad that you've lost, and you'll want to rush everything. Also, for stopping skillers, my advice would be to back off! I'd say bait them, so pretend that you're going to go and tackle them, and then back off! I think a lot of casual players start rushing when I do skills!"

TOM LEESE

TOM SAYS: "I'll give you two tips on how to improve on Weekend League! First, I'd recommend watching players that you know are better than you to help improve. I'd also say learn as many skill moves as possible, especially the four and five-star skills! They'll definitely help to make you unpredictable going forward, as well as making the game more fun!"

JOSEPH HEALY

JOSEPH SAYS: "One thing that has helped me has been watching my gameplay back! There are also a lot of coaching channels now on YouTube that point you in the right direction and they have helped me get to where I am!"

MARC MARLEY

MARC SAYS: "Don't get angry at the game! One loss on Weekend League can turn into five in the space of an hour, so make sure you take plenty of breaks and that you're in the right mindset. Also, I'd say be aggressive in defence, especially with your player switching. You can get punished for being too passive!"

MITCH HAYWARD

MITCH SAYS: "If you really want to improve then your best chance of doing that is by watching players that are better than you. It's all about trying to implement the small details in your game, and eventually those things will stick!"

RYAN PESSOA

RYAN SAYS: "Take it a bit easier when going forward! You don't have to score with every attack instantly. You can take your time. If there's no space, you don't need to force a pass. You can just walk around the midfield a bit, wait for the opposition to pull a defender or midfielder out, and then you can build up through that. Wait for the defender to make a mistake and then pounce on it!"

SHELLZZ

SHELLZZ SAYS: "My one tip to casual players is to learn how to master attacking. It's all about scoring goals and there are so many ways to do that. Stepovers used to be the most important thing in the game. Now you have to know how to use the new bridge skill move, learn how to trigger runs for through balls and maybe use the player lock in certain situations!"

KEIRA WALSH... ULTIMATE GUIDE!

The awesome MAN. CITY and ENGLAND midfielder chats to MATCH about life on and off the pitch!

FAVE ALL-TIME PLAYER!

KEIRA SAYS: "My favourite player is David Silva! Ever since I watched him play for Man. City, even now, he's still my favourite player even though he doesn't play for City anymore. He's somebody that I've always watched and tried to emulate a little bit in my game. He was just incredible, unbelievable!"

LOL SUPERSTITION!

KEIRA SAYS: "One of my superstitions before a game is that I always put my shinpads on the opposite leg, so I don't put them on the one they're supposed to be on! I have no idea why I just started doing it. I can imagine it seems different and not many people do it, but it's just something I've always done and it's stuck with me!"

FIRST LIVE GAME!

KEIRA SAYS: "My dad used to take me to quite a lot of City games! The one that I remember more than any was when we were sat up in the really high stands in the Etihad when City played Arsenal. We'd just signed Emmanuel Adebayor and he scored an unbelievable goal and ran the whole length of the pitch to celebrate in front of the Arsenal fans. It was so funny!"

MAJOR TOURNAMENT EXPERIENCE!

KEIRA SAYS: "Being selected in the squad for any international tournament and being part of such a special group is just an unbelievable feeling. Not many people can say they've gone to the World Cup and the Olympics! As soon as you get that email through that you have been selected, it's such a weight off your shoulders and the best feeling in the world!"

FAVOURITE POSSESSION!

KEIRA SAYS: "It's still related to football! It's the shirt that I wore on my debut for England! It's framed and it's hanging up at my grandma and grandad's house. That's definitely my most prized possession!"

OTHER HOBBIES?

KEIRA SAYS: "I used to play badminton when I was younger. That was probably my second sport. We used to have competitions up and down the country and I used to have lessons. Football was always my main sport, but if I didn't have that I'd probably be playing badminton. In the off-season I'll play as a way of keeping fit but I'm not at my peak!"

FAVE FOOD!

KEIRA SAYS: "It's Chinese and Japanese food! I quite like sushi – I never used to but I do now! When I was younger, the thought of raw fish just didn't appeal to me but as you get older your tastebuds change. A lot of the girls eat it and I had to go along with it. I tried it and I liked it – especially the ones like crispy shrimp. Any Chinese food, I'll eat it!"

FAVE FILM!

KEIRA SAYS: "Notting Hill! It's a classic, isn't it? Ever since I was young it's been my favourite film. I must have watched it over 100 times! I know pretty much all of the lines. I'm probably quite annoying to sit and watch it with, as I'll speak at the same time as them so it can get pretty irritating! I've not known anyone not to like it and I do love a good rom-com!"

TEAM-MATES!

Keira chats about some of her City and England team-mates!

THE DJ!

KEIRA SAYS: "**Chloe Kelly** is the DJ at the minute but when she isn't at the games it is Alex Greenwood. Chloe plays a lot of grime and R'n'B, which I can get on board with, and Alex plays a bit of everything!"

BEST TRAINER!

KEIRA SAYS: "I'd say **Lucy Bronze**, definitely! No matter if it's the warm-up or whatever, she's just so competitive and can't stand losing. You can see that when she plays in the matches as well!"

THE FUNNIEST!

KEIRA SAYS: "**Jill Scott** is definitely the funniest! No matter if it was at City or England, she's just so relaxed, dancing, body popping and it takes everyone else's nerves away, which is important to have before a big game!"

THE LOUDEST!

KEIRA SAYS: "**Georgia Stanway** is definitely the loudest! I can hear her sometimes when I'm eating breakfast before she's even in the room. Even on the pitch, she's the loudest!"

SOCIAL-MEDIA MAD!

KEIRA SAYS: "Probably teenager **Ruby Mace**. I don't actually have TikTok, but she posts on there quite a lot from what I've heard and she's on Instagram too. She's a bit crazy on the social media side!"

BRAINBOX!

KEIRA SAYS: "**Esme Morgan** is quite a brainbox! She uses a lot of intelligent words and she's quite eloquent, so she's definitely up there with being the smartest – and she'd be quite happy to take that title as well!"

MOST FASHIONABLE!

KEIRA SAYS: "I got asked this question before and a few of the girls weren't happy that I didn't say them! I'd say goalkeeper **Ellie Roebuck** or Lucy Bronze. Ellie is so comfortable in her own style and isn't bothered what anyone else thinks as long as she likes it. I can appreciate that in someone else's style!"

MATCH! CHATS TO THE STARS!

MATCH chatted to tons of football superstars during the 2021-22 season! Get a load of the best quotes that featured in our magazine over the past 12 months...

RACHEL FURNESS

We asked what it meant to become Northern Ireland's all-time record goalscorer...

RACHEL SAYS: "It was amazing! The fact my team-mates were just as happy speaks volumes. They know how much I've been through as a player, the injuries I've had, how hard I've had to work. Obviously it's an individual tally, but one I wouldn't have achieved without my team-mates. I hope that I can score many more!"

BEN DAVIES

We asked the Tottenham and Wales hero what his fave other sports are...

BEN SAYS: "Rugby or cricket. Rugby because I was born into it in the Welsh valleys, so I absolutely loved it when I was younger, while I also played cricket locally growing up. I played rugby at county level too, but I had to make a decision between football and rugby and I think I made the right one!"

TRENT ALEXANDER-ARNOLD

MATCH asked the Liverpool full-back who the best team in the world is right now...

TRENT SAYS: "It's very close! You can choose who you want to choose on that topic, really. For us, we see ourselves as being up there - definitely up there - it would be silly not to. We know the quality we've got, but I think Man. City have as well!"

BEN FOSTER

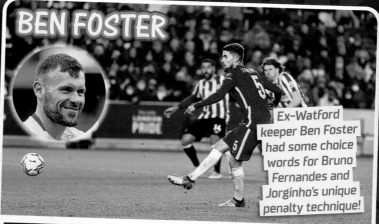

Ex-Watford keeper Ben Foster had some choice words for Bruno Fernandes and Jorginho's unique penalty technique!

BEN SAYS: "Definitely don't do what Bruno Fernandes or Jorginho do! It's the riskiest penalty in the world. If I was the manager and my player took a penalty like that, well, they wouldn't be taking penalties for me! I want my players to run up and hit it 90% power and into a corner-ish. The fancy hop-step-jump is not for me!"

SIMONE MAGILL

We asked the Northern Ireland striker what her favourite animal is...

SIMONE SAYS: "Dogs, 100%, because I've got a little pug called Paddy - it was his third birthday earlier this year! He's more famous than me! He's got Instagram, he's on TikTok and everything - he's got 2,000 or so followers. I was really hot on it when I first got him, but it's hard to keep that up. I just haven't got the time!"

PHIL FODEN

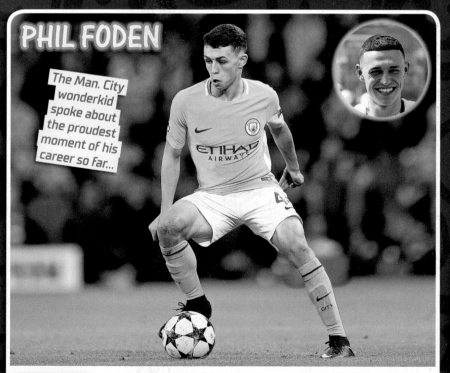

The Man. City wonderkid spoke about the proudest moment of his career so far...

PHIL SAYS: "It's hard to choose one particular moment! Making my debut for City was an incredible moment as someone who had grown up as a fan of the club. Scoring my first goal and being able to celebrate in front of our travelling fans was really special and then obviously we've won trophies and I've played for England, which are things I'm really proud of at this age!"

LAUREN HEMP

We asked the Man. City and England winger for an unknown fact about herself...

LAUREN SAYS: "When I was about six years old, my sister pushed me off a trampoline and I broke my arm! I actually can't touch my shoulder with my left hand anymore, it's impossible for me!"

PATSON DAKA

The Leicester striker revealed he gets extra buzzed when he faces the club he supported as a child, Liverpool...

PATSON SAYS: "Playing against them, wow, I don't know how to describe the feeling. I felt more connected playing against a club that I grew up supporting. I just wanted to make it a memorable moment, because I never imagined it would come so quick!"

ELLEN WHITE

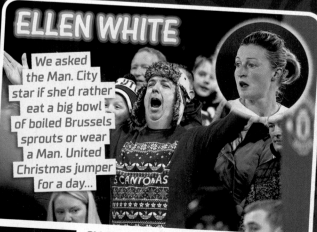

We asked the Man. City star if she'd rather eat a big bowl of boiled Brussels sprouts or wear a Man. United Christmas jumper for a day...

ELLEN SAYS: "Definitely Brussels sprouts, 100%! I don't mind them, so that's an easy one for me. I couldn't be seen in a Man. United jumper. I love December because I can just wear a Christmas jumper with jeans and that's my outfit. I need to buy a City one!"

EURO 2022 Scrapbook!

MINI CAR RETURNS!

The mini car that became world-famous after bringing the match ball to the centre-circle for the kick-off of the men's 2020 European Championship made a return at Old Trafford for England's opener against Austria!

AND WE'RE OFF!

The first goal of the tournament came from Lionesses and Arsenal winger Beth Mead against Austria, as she lobbed the ball over her Gunners team-mate Manuela Zinsberger's head!

EURO DEBUTANTS!

Northern Ireland made their Euros debut against Norway! The result didn't go their way but Julie Nelson became a history maker as she scored the nation's first-ever goal on the European stage!

TERRIFIC TREBLE!

France got their campaign off to the perfect start with a 5-1 demolition of Italy, but the star of the show was midfielder Grace Geyoro! She became the first player in Women's Euros history to net a first-half hat-trick!

FAST START!

Finland's Linda Sallstrom was fast out the blocks against Spain, busting the net after just 50 seconds! Unfortunately for her side, they still went on to lose 4-1!

THUNDERCLAP!

Even though there were less than 4,000 supporters in attendance for Iceland's game against Belgium, it felt more like 40,000! The atmosphere was immense, and we also got to see the famous Thunderclap again!

CRAZY COMEBACK!

The best comeback of the group stage happened when Portugal took on Switzerland! The Swiss were two goals ahead after just five minutes, but Portugal scored two second-half goals to complete the comeback!

LETHAL LIONESSES!

England set a new record for the biggest margin of victory at a Women's Euros with their 8-0 annihilation of Norway, overtaking their own record from the 2017 edition!

ROCKING RECORD!

Euro 2022 shattered the record for the total attendance at a Women's European Championship while still being in the group stage! The 8,173 who watched France beat Belgium 2-1 at Rotherham's New York Stadium took the Euros to a total of 248,075 fans!

SUPER SUB!

Alessia Russo became only the third substitute to score two goals in a Women's Euros game in the all-UK clash against Northern Ireland! Her first came just 132 seconds after coming onto the pitch!

NORTHERN IRELAND BOW OUT!

Northern Ireland's group-stage exit didn't stop them from partying with their supporters at the end of their final game in one of the most heart-warming moments of the tourno! They should still be proud!

EURO 2022 Scrapbook!

STOP THE CLOCK!

France v Iceland not only had the earliest goal of the tournament after just 46 seconds from Melvine Malard, it also had the latest with Dagny Brynjarsdottir converting a penalty in the 12th minute of stoppage-time!

FANTASTIC FIVE!

Ruthless Sweden marched into the quarter-finals after scoring five times against Portugal in the group stage – their joint-biggest win in Women's Euros history!

HISTORY MAKERS!

Belgium reached the quarter-finals of the Women's Euros for the first time ever after overcoming Italy in a tense Group D finale at Manchester's Academy Stadium!

STANWAY'S STUNNER!

England's quarter-final with Spain was a tight, tense affair that was ultimately settled by Georgia Stanway's extra-time scorcher! Her missile also marked England's 100th goal under manager Sarina Wiegman. Awesome!

POPP GOES THE AUSTRIA!

Germany edged out Austria 2-0 to reach the semi-finals, and Alexandra Popp was once again the star as she became only the second player in Women's Euros history to score in four games in a row!

FRANCE BREAK CURSE!

France's massive quarter-final clash with the Netherlands was a mouth-watering head-to-head between two of the tournament's heavyweights! Les Bleues finally ended their quarter-final hoodoo by winning their first-ever knockout match at the Women's Euros!

LAST-GASP GLORY!

Sweden huffed and puffed against underdogs Belgium in their quarter-final before Linda Sembrant finally found a way through in the 90th minute – with what was their 33rd shot of the match!

THE RUSSO SHOW!

England smashed Sweden 4-0 in their semi-final in Sheffield, but the moment of the match was an outrageous piece of skill from Russo – the super sub produced a jaw-dropping backheel to nutmeg the keeper! Cue Sweet Caroline on repeat and a place in the final booked!

DEADLY DOUBLE!

Germany and France's mammoth semi-final didn't quite live up to the pre-match hype! That didn't stop Germany goal machine Popp from stealing the headlines as she scored a brace to clinch her side a place in the final at Wembley!

EXTRA-TIME DRAMA IN THE FINAL!

England thought they'd wrapped up the final after substitute Ella Toone's exquisite lob, but Germany's equaliser through Lina Magull took the game to extra-time. It was then that Chloe Kelly stabbed the all-important winner from close range, sparking crazy celebrations – on the pitch and in the stands!

FOOTBALL CAME HOME!

England's trophy lift in front of a European Championship record attendance was a poetic end to the competition for Three Lions fans – it marked the nation's first major tournament victory since beating Germany at Wembley in 1966!

MAGIC MEAD!

They say the perfect photo doesn't exist but Beth Mead posing with a Euros winners' medal, the top goalscorer award and the Player of the Tournament prize is as near to perfection as you'll get!

BIG MATCH QUIZ!

How many of these mega tough WSL teasers can you get right?

WHO STARTED WHERE?

Which clubs did these superstars start their senior career with?

VICKY LOSADA	MELANIE LEUPOLZ	VIVIANNE MIEDEMA	KIRSTY HANSON	MAEVA CLEMARON	INESSA KAAGMAN
 1	 2	 3	 4	 5	 6

A	B	C	D	E	F
 FREIBURG	 SC HEERENVEEN	 SHEFFIELD FC	 AJAX	 BARCELONA	 SAINT-ETIENNE

ODD ONE OUT!

 LIVERPOOL

 MAN. UNITED

 ARSENAL

 NOTTS COUNTY

Which of these clubs has England defender Alex Greenwood not played for during her quality career?

THEY SAID WHAT?

Which superstar made this funny comment?

"I was in a school performance once, but I was in the background and strumming very lightly!"

A. Lauren Hemp

B. Sam Kerr

C. Simone Magill

LIST IT! ✓

Put two minutes on a timer and list ten England stars playing in the WSL!

 _____
 _____
 _____
 _____
 _____
 _____
_____
_____
_____
_____

ACE ACTIVITY

WORDFIT

Fit these awesome Women's Super League stars into the giant grid below!

Anvegard	Fleming	Kiernan	Moloney	Shaw
Ayane	Hampton	Losada	Ouahabi	Spencer
Cuthbert	Harder	McCabe	Perisset	Svitkova
Dowie	Kerr	Miedema	Rose	Williams

ANSWERS ON PAGE 94

FOOTY'S FUNNIEST MEMES!

MATCH picks out some of the best footy memes from social media!

NO ENTRY!

Whenever a team lets in a proper dodgy goal or has a defensive nightmare, this useless gate meme does the rounds. LOL!

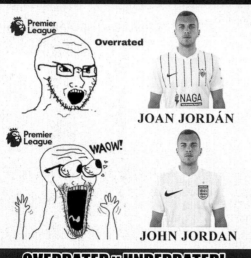

OVERRATED v UNDERRATED!

Spanish side Sevilla actually used this meme in 2022 to have a pop at English players' hype!

MEANS BUSINESS!

This FIFA-inspired meme appears when a player or team turns up the heat in a match!

THE CARRIERS!

This LOL meme was from 2021-22, but gets used whenever two players carry their team!

I KNOW THAT FEEL BRO

I KNOW THAT FEEL, BRO!

When two teams go on to lose to the same opponent, this hugging embrace is always used!

NEYMAR WAKING UP ON HIS BIRTHDAY

THEN GOING ON SOCIAL MEDIA TO SEE ALL THE MESSAGES FOR RONALDO

BIRTHDAY PAIN!

This Neymar-Ronaldo birthday meme re-emerges on February 5 every year without fail!

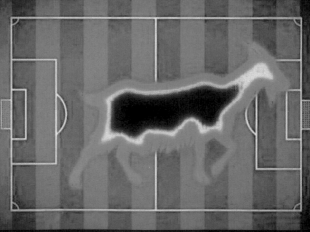

THE G.O.A.T!

This famous "GOAT" heat map is used whenever a player drops a 10/10 worldie performance!

WE HAVE A HOUSE RIGHT UP YOUR STREET!

I'VE GOT THE X-TRACTOR, MATCH!

ERLING HAALAND
FARMER
We know Haaland had a go at rapping when he was younger, but he also spends time on a potato farm with his father during the summer holidays! "Smashing"!

sold

MOHAMED SALAH
ESTATE AGENT
Imagine being shown around a house by the classy Liverpool forward! He actually owns his own estate agents in London, but we reckon the places are probably pretty expensive...

FOOTY STARS'

Here's what some stars would be doing if they weren't professional footballers...

HOW CAN I HELP YOU TODAY?

MAZ PACHECO
LAWYER
She grew up watching crime shows on the TV and ended up graduating with a degree in law, so we can definitely imagine the Aston Villa defender locking up loads of baddies!

LADIES AND GENTS OF THE JURY...

GABBY GEORGE
SHOP ASSISTANT
The Everton and England defender says she wanted to be a shopkeeper so she could sit at a till and scan all of the items! She must have been over-the-moon when self checkout was invented!

SIX MORE LAPS, GUYS!

DELE ALLI
P.E. TEACHER
The classy midfielder revealed to MATCH back in 2020 that if he wasn't a footballer, he'd probably be a P.E. teacher! To be fair, we wouldn't mind being taught some top tricks by Dele!

MICHAIL ANTONIO
LIFEGUARD

NO DIVING IN THE SHALLOW END!

The West Ham forward never feels "out of depth" in the Premier League, because he used to be a part-time lifeguard! Apparently he never had to dive in to rescue anybody, though!

ROSELLA AYANE
BRAIN SURGEON

LET'S SCRUB IN!

The Tottenham forward grew up dreaming of becoming a brain surgeon! If she wasn't a footballer, she reckons she definitely would have become a doctor at least!

RAHEEM STERLING
FASHION DESIGNER

SLICK THREADS ALERT!

Tons of football stars love fashion, but not many have their own clothing range! Razza released his debut line called 1692 in 2021, so could we see him rivalling the likes of Armani in the future?

GERARD PIQUE
POKER PLAYER

FULL HOUSE!

The Barcelona defender is a huge fan of card game Poker! In fact, he once won over £500,000 at an event, so he could definitely make a living out of the game!

OTHER JOBS!

NEYMAR
ACTOR

JUST GIMME THE ACADEMY AWARD ALREADY!

The sick skiller loves being the centre of attention, so it would make sense for him to be an actor! He actually made a cameo appearance as a monk in a famous 2019 Spanish TV series!

ROBERT LEWANDOWSKI
VIDEO GAME CREATOR

The Poland hitman actually already has his own video games company, known as RL9.Games! He released his first game in 2021, which was a mix between FIFA and Football Manager!

LEVEL UP!

GOAL KING #4
MBAPPE

PSG and FRANCE's fabulous forward has been tearing defences apart for so long, it's easy to forget he's still only 23! There's plenty more to come from KYLIAN MBAPPE!

GOALSCORING GAME

✓ Mbappe is insanely quick, so loads of his goals come from simply burning past defenders and lashing the ball in. He's uncatchable!

✓ He's not just a speed merchant, though – Kylian has ice-cool composure and world-class technique, so he always picks the right finish!

✓ His versatility makes him a huge threat too! He can play on either wing or up front, and gets tons of goals cutting in off the wing!

LAST SEASON

Mbappe won the Ligue 1 Golden Boot for the fourth year in a row in 2021-22 – the first player to do so in 30 years! Alongside his 28 league goals, he also topped the assist charts with 17, and bagged six in the Champions League – ending with 39 in all comps – while also hitting the winner in the UEFA Nations League final for France!

BREAKTHROUGH SEASON

Defences all across Europe were blown away by a teenage wonderkid when Mbappe first burst onto the scene in 2016-17! His combination of explosive pace and fearless dribbling helped Monaco bag a stunning Ligue 1 title and reach the Champions League semis, beating Man. City along the way!

FACTPACK!

Club: *PSG*
Country: *France*
Age: *23*
Height: *5ft 10in*
Top Skill: *Lightning speed!*

STAT PACK

42 — Mbappe's best scoring season was in 2020-21, when he banged in 42 goals in just 47 games!

2 — Last season Mbappe overtook Zlatan Ibrahimovic to become PSG's second-highest scorer of all time!

30 — He's the youngest player to score 30 CL goals, overtaking Lionel Messi's record!

19 — In 2018 he became the youngest player to score for France at a World Cup, aged 19, and fired them to glory with four goals!

GREATEST GOAL

PSG	1	0	Real Madrid

February 15, 2022 It looked like Mbappe was going nowhere when he picked up the ball in the dying seconds of this game, then all of a sudden he'd tied the full-back in knots and slotted home!

WHAT'S NEXT?

After turning down Real Madrid to sign a new contract at PSG, Mbappe has his sights on one thing only - winning the Champo League with the French giants! He's also coming for Edinson Cavani's record of 200 goals for the club, and should definitely overtake him by the end of 2023!

Stats correct up to start of the 2022-23 season.

SHOCKING SITTERS!

DON'T TRY THESE AT HOME!

MATCH re-visits some of the worst misses in footy history! Scan the QR codes to watch 'em!

▶ ▶| 1:35 / 8:12   HD ◀» ⌄⌄

▶ RONNY ROSENTHAL

ASTON VILLA v LIVERPOOL, 1992

One of the Premier League's worst-ever misses actually happened in its first-ever season! Liverpool's Israeli striker Ronny Rosenthal did all the hard work by rounding the Villa goalkeeper but, with just an open goal in front of him, overcooked his shot and hit the crossbar. Ouch!

▶ ▶| 1:35 / 8:12   HD ◀» ⌄⌄

▶ ERIC MAXIM CHOUPO-MOTING

PSG v STRASBOURG, 2018

We think everybody was a bit surprised when PSG signed Choupo-Moting from Stoke, but nobody could have imagined this miss! We're not sure if it even counts as a "miss", because he actually stops his team-mate's shot from crossing the line, knocking it against the post from just a yard out!

▶ ▶| 1:35 / 8:12   HD ◀» ⌄⌄

▶ ARNALDO VERA

LIBERTAD v EMELEC, 2003

Over to South America now for this mind-boggling fail from the Copa Libertadores! After nicking the ball past the goalkeeper, Paraguayan Vera shins it onto the crossbar from one yard out. The only (tiny) excuse we can think of is that he was a centre-back! Luckily, his side won the game 5-1!

▶ ▶| 1:35 / 8:12   HD ◀» ⌄⌄

▶ FERNANDO TORRES

MAN. UNITED v CHELSEA, 2011

Spanish striker Torres made a name for himself as one of the finest finishers in England during his time at Liverpool, but this sitter summed up his spell at Chelsea! He rounded Man. United's David de Gea but skewed his shot wide to the relief of the Old Trafford crowd! It was on his weaker left foot, but surely that's no excuse?

▶ ▶| 1:35 / 8:12   HD ◀» ⌄⌄

▶ ASTER VRANCKX

MECHELEN v KV OOSTENDE, 2020

Once you've watched this clip, you'll be asking yourself if ex-Mechelen midfielder Vranckx was wearing high heels rather than football boots! He got his legs in a right tangle on the goal-line and ended up treading on the ball rather than side-footing it home - finishing on his backside and with the ball going out for a goal kick. Fail!

KLOSE

1 The German is the all-time top scorer in men's World Cup history with how many goals – 16, 18 or 20?

2 Which edition of the World Cup did he win the Golden Boot with five goals – 2006, 2010 or 2014?

3 True or False? Germany never lost a single game in which Klose scored between 2001 and 2014!

4 He's also Germany's all-time top scorer with how many international goals – 60, 71 or 93?

5 Which huge Italian team did he end his career at – Roma, AC Milan, Inter, Lazio, Juventus or Fiorentina?

ANSWERS ON PAGE 94

FIRST MEETING

Guardiola's first-ever game against Klopp was also his first game in German footy as Bayern Munich faced Borussia Dortmund in the German Super Cup. The curtain-raiser for 2013-14 was an absolute cracker – Klopp's Dortmund welcomed Pep to Germany with an awesome 4-2 win, with future Man. City midfielder Ilkay Gundogan among the goals!

SIGN ME UP, PEP!

FIRST TITLE

Pep and Bayern didn't have to wait long to get their revenge. A few months later they dominated in Dortmund with a 3-0 victory thanks to Arjen Robben, Thomas Muller and ex-Dortmund star Mario Gotze! Klopp's men did win by the same scoreline in Munich, but by then Pep had already sealed his first Bundesliga title!

KLOPP v

I'M THE BEST!

LEWA SWOOP

Guardiola's next big victory against Klopp came off the pitch, as Bayern snapped up Dortmund's star striker Robert Lewandowski on a free transfer in 2014! That season he grabbed the winner in a 1-0 win against Klopp's men – the first of 27 goals that he has scored against his old club. Wowzers!

SEE YA, GUYS – I'M OFF!

BYE-BYE BUNDESLIGA

The 2014-15 season turned out to be Klopp's final campaign in Dortmund, as he struggled to a disappointing seventh place, while Pep won his second Bundesliga in a row. The German still had time for one last victory over his rival though, as his side defeated Bayern in the semi-finals of the German Cup on penalties!

PREM REUNION

Klopp moved to Liverpool in October 2015, and the following summer Pep joined him in England by taking charge of Man. City. All eyes were on Anfield for their first Prem meeting at the end of 2016, and Liverpool nicked it 1-0 thanks to a header from Dutchman Gini Wijnaldum!

PEP

2023 marks the ten-year anniversary of PEP GUARDIOLA and JURGEN KLOPP's first-ever clash! MATCH has been taking a look back through the history of this epic managerial rivalry...

FIVE-STAR CITY

Liverpool's trip to the Etihad at the start of 2017-18 was expected to be another close clash, but it turned into an absolute demolition job! The Reds started well but collapsed after forward Sadio Mane was sent off for a dangerous high challenge on Ederson, and City ran riot in a 5-0 win!

Speech bubble: RED SUITS ME WAY BETTER!

VAN DIJK ARRIVES

Klopp and Guardiola went head-to-head in the transfer market again in the 2017-18 season, with both men chasing Southampton centre-back Virgil van Dijk. The Dutchman eventually joined Liverpool and has gone on to become one of the PL's greatest defenders, and later admitted that Klopp convinced him to turn down City!

ANFIELD EPIC

Pep arrived at Anfield in January 2018 well on the way to his first Premier League title, but Klopp's deadly front three of Roberto Firmino, Sadio Mane and Mohamed Salah blew City away! The trio were all on target as Liverpool won 4-3, with the visitors scoring twice late on!

CHAMPIONS LEAGUE SHOWDOWNS

The rivalry between the managerial masters was dialled up when they met in the Champions League quarter-finals! Liverpool's Anfield magic made the difference, as they scored three goals in 31 minutes in the first leg, before The Reds sealed their place in the semis with a 2-1 win at the Etihad a week later!

Speech bubble: TAKE THAT, KLOPP!

EPIC TITLE RACE

Although City won the 2017-18 title, Liverpool ended strongly and went into the next season ready to take them on. In the most epic title race of all time, The Reds racked up 97 points in 2018-19 and only lost once all season – but that solitary 2-1 defeat at the Etihad made the difference, as City won the league by just one point!

LOCKDOWN LEAGUE

The Reds were seriously fired up for 2019-20! After beating City 3-1 in November, they went nine points clear of their rivals at the top of the Prem and were cruising to the title! COVID interrupted the season, but in the end Klopp made history as the first man to bring the Premier League trophy to Anfield!

WE'RE HISTORY MAKERS, GUYS!

ANFIELD ANNIHILATION

Klopp spent most of 2020-21 with a selection headache after COVID and injuries hit his squad hard. He had to pick midfielders Jordan Henderson and Fabinho at centre-back for Man. City's visit to Anfield in February, and Pep's men tore them to shreds with a 4-1 win before reclaiming their Premier League crown!

HEAD-TO-HEAD

The two men have lost more games to each other than against any other manager! In 24 meetings before the start of the 2022-23 season, Klopp won ten games and Pep won nine, with five draws!

CLASH OF STYLES

One of the things that makes this rivalry so good is the different tactics of the coaches. Pep likes his teams to boss possession and play out from the back, but that always come under severe pressure from Klopp's insane 'gegenpressing' style!

TROPHY COUNT

When it comes to honours, Pep is miles ahead of Klopp with 33 career trophies compared to 12. The German has one thing Guardiola doesn't have, though - a Champions League trophy with his English club!

RIVALRY RENEWED

Klopp and Pep led the league again in 2021-22, and for the second time in three years the title race went all the way down to the final day of the season. Once again, City edged it by a single point, but Klopp did at least win the Carabao Cup, and then the FA Cup, beating Pep's side 3-2 in the semi-finals!

MY ARMS ARE ACHING!

WHAT'S NEXT?

Klopp recently signed a contract keeping him in England until 2026, and Guardiola is expected to sign a similar deal, so there should be plenty more to come in this epic rivalry! We can't wait!

WHO'S YOUR EURO TEAM?

WHO'S YOUR SECOND TEAM?

Which team outside the Premier League from Europe's top five leagues should you support? Take our test to find out...

WINNERS
UEFA CHAMPIONS LEAGUE 2021/2022

1

WINNING MENTALITY?

Is winning more important to you than anything else?

| ✓ | If Yes, go to question 2! |
| ✗ | If No, go to question 4! |

STYLE OF FOOTBALL!

Does your team need to boss possession in every single match?

2

| ✓ | If Yes, go to question 3! |
| ✗ | If No, go to question 7! |

3

NEYMAR JR 10

BIG-NAME TRANSFERS!

Do you want your team to buy only the biggest names available?

| ✓ | If Yes, go to question 5! |
| ✗ | If No, go to question 8! |

4

BRITISH PLAYER?

Do you want your team to have a British player in their squad?

| ✓ | If Yes, go to question 6! |
| ✗ | If No, go to question 9! |

5 EUROPEAN HISTORY?

Does your team need to have won tons of European titles in the past?

| ✓ | If Yes, you should support Real Madrid! |
| ✗ | If No, you should support PSG! |

6 ANIMAL MASCOT?

Would you prefer your club's mascot to be an animal?

| ✓ | If Yes, you should support Roma! |
| ✗ | If No, you should support Milan! |

7 GROUND-SHARING?

Do you mind sharing your stadium with a massive rival?

| ✓ | If Yes, you should support Atletico Madrid! |
| ✗ | If No, you should support Inter! |

CRISTIANO CONNECTION?

Do you want your team to be associated with Cristiano Ronaldo?

| ✓ | If Yes, you should support Juventus! |
| ✗ | If No, you should support Bayern Munich! |

8

9 SHIRT DESIGN!

Do you want your home shirt to have stripes?

| ✓ | If Yes, go to question 10! |
| ✗ | If No, you should support Bayer Leverkusen! |

10 HOT OR COLD?

Do you prefer it to be hot when you go to a football match?

| ✓ | If Yes, you should support Real Betis! |
| ✗ | If No, you should support Hertha Berlin! |

EACH CONTINENT'S
MOST VALUABLE

NORTH & CENTRAL AMERICA

USA

VALUE: £185 MILLION

The USA's squad has a young average age, so their combined value is definitely on the up! Their two most valuable players are forwards **Christian Pulisic** and **Giovanni Reyna**, but the likes of **Tyler Adams**, **Yunus Musah**, **Gianluca Busio** and **Ricardo Pepi** are young talents whose prices are skyrocketing!

EUROPE

ENGLAND

VALUE: £940 MILLION

Officially the most valuable national team in the world, it's no surprise that Gareth Southgate has such a headache picking his starting XI! Three Lions skipper **Harry Kane** is the highest-valued player in the squad, with **Phil Foden** second on the list. France's jaw-dropping squad is just below The Three Lions in the value charts!

USA vs URUGUAY

JUNE 5, 2022
KANSAS CITY, KS

Allstate

SOUTH AMERICA

BRAZIL

VALUE: £765 MILLION

Brazil and Argentina are mega fierce rivals but the Samba Stars come out on top in this battle! Forwards **Neymar** and **Vinicius Junior** are worth close to £200 million alone, while the likes of **Eder Militao**, **Gabriel Martinelli** and **Antony** are stars with rising stock. We wouldn't be surprised to see them overtake England in the future!

ELIMINATÓRIAS
Copa do Mundo FIFA Catar 2022™

AFRICA

SENEGAL

VALUE: £298 MILLION

The most valuable player in the Senegal squad is **Sadio Mane**, but the likes of **Kalidou Koulibaly**, **Edouard Mendy** and **Ismaila Sarr** also keep the Lions of Teranga at the top! Ivory Coast are just behind them, which is why it was such a shock they didn't even qualify for the 2022 World Cup!

NATIONAL TEAMS!

The combined value of the players in these national team squads is higher than any other country on their continent!

ASIA
SOUTH KOREA
VALUE: £120 MILLION

There's one main reason why South Korea are Asia's most valuable nation and his name is Heung-Min Son! The Tottenham star and Korea captain is a proper fans' favourite at club and international level, while Wolves ace Hee-Chan Hwang is hoping to follow in Sonny's footsteps by having as much of an impact on the Premier League!

OCEANIA
NEW ZEALAND
VALUE: £21 MILLION

Half of New Zealand's total squad value is made up of Newcastle striker **Chris Wood**, with only two other players valued at over £1 million – Brondby baller **Joe Bell** and Empoli full-back **Liberato Cacace**. The Magpies targetman became his nation's all-time record goalscorer in March 2022 and is the best-ever Kiwi to play in England!

MAP KEY

AFC
Asian Football Confederation

CAF
Confédération Africaine de Football

CONCACAF
Confederation of North, Central American & Caribbean Association Football

CONMEBOL
Confederación Sudamericana de Fútbol

UEFA
Union of European Football Associations

OFC
Oceania Football Confederation

N/A
No affiliation

GOAL KING #5
SALAH

After joining LIVERPOOL back in 2017, MOHAMED SALAH went from being a quick and tricky winger to one of the planet's most prolific goalscorers – and on his way to becoming a Prem legend!

GOALSCORING GAME

✓ Salah's best position is on the right side of attack, and he's at his most dangerous when cutting inside onto his lethal left foot!

✓ He's a nightmare to defend against because he makes loads of runs in behind the defence, but he's just as dangerous when dribbling!

✓ Nobody took more shots than Salah in the 2021-22 Prem season, so he's always threatening to find the back of the net!

BEST SEASON

Salah has been Liverpool's top goalscorer every season since he arrived, but his best campaign was his first. The Egyptian king racked up record-breaking numbers on his way to the Prem Golden Boot and Champions League final, smashing home 44 goals in all comps. Wow!

Club: *Liverpool*
Country: *Egypt*
Age: *30*
Height: *5ft 9in*
Top Skill: *Epic dribbling!*

FACTPACK!

STAT PACK

36 Salah was directly involved in 36 Prem goals in 2021-22 – more than any other player!

3 The Liverpool star has three Prem Golden Boots – only Thierry Henry has more!

32 He still holds the record for the most goals in a 38-game Prem season in 2017-18!

151 It only took him 151 games to score 100 PL goals for Liverpool – quicker than anyone in the club's history!

LAST SEASON

Salah started 2021-22 in unstoppable form! In October he became the first Liverpool player to score in ten straight games by bagging a hat-trick against arch-rivals Man. United – the first-ever Prem treble by an away player at Old Trafford! His form tailed off after losing the Africa Cup of Nations final with Egypt in February, but he still ended as the Premier League's joint-top goalscorer and top assister. Hero!

GREATEST GOAL

Liverpool	2	2	Man. City

October 3, 2021 Salah won the Premier League Goal of the Season for this stroke of genius! He skipped through the City defence with twinkle toes before finishing with his weaker right foot!

WHAT'S NEXT?

Last summer, Salah ended gossip about his future by signing a new contract with Liverpool, so he's fully focused on success at Anfield! The Egypt star was gutted to miss out on the World Cup, but the good news for The Reds is that he'll get a rest in the middle of the campaign so should be in top form all season long!

Stats correct up to start of the 2022-23 season.

FIFA WORLD CUP QATAR 2022™

ADRENALYN XL FROM PANINI

As ever, where there's football and the FIFA World Cup™, there's also Panini, so get ready to kick off with FIFA World Cup Qatar 2022™ Adrenalyn XL™, the official card collection that gets bigger and better with every edition!

HEROES

The HEROES cards are the heart of the collection, which you can slot into your Collector's Album around their TEAM CRESTS, representing each national side!

SPECIALS

These totally jaw-dropping cards make this collection extra special! They include the traditional FANS' FAVOURITES - the players who the supporters can't get enough of; TOP KEEPERS - the best goalies; TITANS - the most rock-solid defenders; MAGICIANS - the midfield masters; and GOAL MACHINES - the best strikers on the planet. Get in there!

NEW

There's also cool, brand-new cards featuring FIFA World Cup™ newbies and champions of the tournament - the ROOKIES and LEGENDS! Who will you get?

CONTENDERS

Especially for this tournament, Panini have also added the CONTENDERS and CONTENDER TEAMS cards, representing the national teams that took part in the play-offs!

RARES

Watch out for the strongest cards of all - the TOP MASTERS - a must-have card for any Adrenalyn XL™ fan, and the super-rare INVINCIBLES, the collection's most-wanted card!

Bust open your packets and you might even find some of the incredible, amazing GAME CHANGERS! Plus, with the new rarity icon at the bottom of each card, you can easily identify the most valuable cards in your collection!

WIN!

OFFICIAL FIFA WORLD CUP QATAR 2022™ ADRENALYN XL™ BUNDLE!

Thanks to our mates at Panini, one lucky MATCH reader will win a FIFA World Cup Qatar 2022™ Adrenalyn XL™ Starter Pack, Pocket Tin and Box of 50 Packets!

HOW TO ENTER THIS COMPETITION!

VISIT... WWW.MATCHFOOTBALL.CO.UK

Then click 'WIN' in the navigation bar on the MATCH website. Full terms and conditions are available online
Closing date: January 31, 2023.

The Starter Pack includes a Binder, Gameboard, Game Guide, 3 packets and 1 Limited Edition card!

With 50 packets, you'll get your collection well and truly underway!

The Pocket Tin includes 5 packets and 2 Limited Edition cards!

Bolder and brighter than ever before, FIFA World Cup Qatar 2022™ Adrenalyn XL™ allows you to build your dream team player by player! Play these stunning cards in real-life games against your friends, or use them for Panini's ever-growing online game. Let the adventure begin! Visit panini.co.uk for more information.

PACKED EVERY ISSUE WITH....

MASSIVE STARS

RED-HOT GEAR

ACE INTERVIEWS

EPIC FEATURES

AMAZING POSTERS

TIPS & QUIZZES!

SUBSCRIBE TO MATCH!...

CALL
01959 543 747
QUOTE: MATAN23

ONLINE
SHOP.KELSEY.
CO.UK/MATAN23

QUIZ ANSWERS!

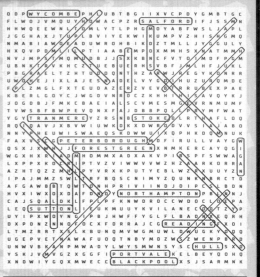

Premier League Quiz · Pages 26-27

Spot The Ball: 5.

Five-A-Side: 1. GK - Lukasz Fabianski;
2. DF - Cristian Romero;
3. RMF - Martin Odegaard;
4. LMF - Enock Mwepu;
5. ST - Chris Wood.

The Price Is Right: 1B; 2A; 3C.

Kit Clash: Daniel Podence.

Face In The Crowd: See above.

Euro Leagues Quiz · Pages 36-37

Name The Team: 1. Thibaut Courtois; 2. David Alaba; 3. Toni Kroos; 4. Eder Militao; 5. Casemiro; 6. Karim Benzema; 7. Lucas Vazquez; 8. Ferland Mendy; 9. Vinicius Junior; 10. Luka Modric.

Baby Face: Antoine Griezmann.

MATCH! Winner: Robert Lewandowski.

Legendary: 1. Barcelona; 2. Inter; 3. Juventus; 4. Real Madrid; 5. AC Milan; 6. Bayern Munich.

Crossword: See right.

One point for each correct answer!
MY SCORE /161

EFL Quiz · Pages 54-55

Soccer Scramble: 1. Chris Willock;
2. Jordan Rhodes; 3. Karlan Grant;
4. Andreas Weimann.

Name The Club: Middlesbrough.

Bogus Badge: Plymouth.

Higher Or Lower?: 1. Higher; 2. Higher;
3. Lower; 4. Lower; 5. Higher.

Wordsearch: See top right.

WSL Quiz · Pages 70-71

Who Started Where?: 1E; 2A; 3B; 4C; 5F; 6D.

Odd One Out: Arsenal.

They Said What?: Simone Magill.

List It: Your score out of 10.

Wordfit: See below.

Quiz Posters

Xavi Quiz:
1. 2000; 2. True; 3. No; 4. Two; 5. Xavi.

David Beckham Quiz:
1. True; 2. Bend It Like Beckham;
3. 59 games; 4. Greece; 5. Wayne Rooney.

Zinedine Zidane Quiz:
1. Brazil; 2. Zizou; 3. False - it was Algeria;
4. adidas Predator; 5. 31 goals.

Ronaldo Quiz: 1. True; 2. Juventus;
3. 2002; 4. 15 goals; 5. Less than 100.

Miroslav Klose Quiz: 1. 16 goals;
2. 2006; 3. True; 4. 71 goals; 5. Lazio.

94 MATCH!